PAVEL BATEL

The Tour guide story

CONTENTS

"Thanks for everything. Please take care of the details as quickly as you can. With luck, everything will go smoothly and I'll have them out soon." Jakob fixes me with a disbelieving look one last time, then turns around and starts running back into the darkness of the tunnel. I crawl through the gap between the wardrobe and the wall to another cellar – the last one. My flashlight illuminates the space and I search for something, anything, that might come in handy. The light seems to be fading: but if the batteries run out I'm going to be leading twenty-seven children through pitch darkness, so I'd better do what I have to quickly and make it back before that happens. At the top of the stairs I find a door, which, unsurprisingly, is locked. Jakob's pick doesn't work for me, but it's no wonder, given the way my hands are shaking. Instead, I pick up the bayonet, a solid piece of iron, and smash it against the lock, which now gives way easily.

Quietly, I enter a small room with windows, dimly lit by the lanterns in the prison yard. As I sneak towards one of the windows I notice a little table with a lamp, next to a narrow couch. Is this a guardroom?

It reminds me of military school, except that we lounged on a ripped-out bathroom door instead of a proper divan. The doors leading out to the yard are open. A guard might come in at any moment, or, he might not, but I'm not going to wait and find out. Taking a deep breath, I head out into the courtyard.

Does my story begin here? Not really; this is neither the beginning nor the end. Walk with me back in time, and help me pick up the fragments and understand it myself.

CHAPTER 1: THE EIGHTIES, THREE YEARS AFTER THE BIG MOVE

Just a little longer and he'll be here. I'm standing with Miky and Mom under the iron horse on Wenceslas Square, waiting for Papa. Three years have passed since we last saw him, but finally things have changed and we can visit Slovakia.

Miky fidgets in his excitement to see our Papa again, but I'm just standing and thinking about what I'm going to say. Am I angry with him? I'm excited to see him, but I'm also upset. Why did he leave me alone in the hospital all alone and never come to visit? Why did he let us go away to Prague and never write? Why...? But, on the other hand, do I want to confront him and spoil our two weeks in paradise? I'm eleven years old and that's how I think of my real home in Slovakia: it's paradise.

"Papa!" Miky is the first one to spot him, and runs into his arms. Papa is moved by this and I can see tears running down his cheeks; just a few, but I can see them. He shakes hands with

Mom and then focuses his attention on me.

"Pauli, hiya son ... Wow, you've grown up ... You both have ..."

He wants to hug me, but I resist, putting out my hand instead.

"Hey, Dad."

The train journey takes five hours and I spend most of it staring out the window. I don't want to be unkind to Papa, but my head still is full of angry questions and I still don't know where or how to begin.

I can feel how sorry he is about the same things I'm mulling over, but that isn't enough, not nearly.

Anyway, we've got two weeks ahead of us to spend together, which leaves plenty of time for all kinds of questions. The tension will have to break and we'll enjoy our time together. He knows that too, which is why he isn't rushing things. Neither of us wants to spoil the vacation.

"Hey there you guys, how's it going? Well, come on in – Julia and the family are already here. Zvalo baked you a cake and we've already started in on her famous plum pie." Aunt Janny opens the doors of her huge, five-room Bratislava apartment, where Grandma, Grandpa, and Uncle Milan also live. We are in for a big surprise: nearly the whole family has gathered together to welcome us.

"We got the boys sandwiches at the station."

"Oh, you shouldn't have – do you know how much food we've made? No one goes hungry here!"

"Come on in, Grandma's telling stories."

Grandma is very sweet (in spite of her quick temper). When it flares up, she usually calms down just as quickly and apologizes to anyone she may have offended. Aunt Julia, a kindergarten teacher, helps me take off my jacket and hangs it on the coatrack.

"Well, Pauli, what's new in Prague?"

"Not much. It's good to see you, Auntie."

"Look at you: you know how to speak Czech now! How did you get those bruises on your hands? Did you get into a fight? You'd better not, or you know the teachers won't like you and they'll get on your case."

"If only you knew, Auntie."

Gosh, how I love Bratislava – and this family that belongs to me, and to which I belong. As I said before: it's paradise. Aunt Janny takes us into the living room. Everyone is here. In the corner, uncle Jaromir is having a passionate political discussion with cousins from Nitra; Grandma is eating a dessert in the armchair; Grandpa is stretched out on the couch, smiling. Cousin Lesana, two years older than me, comes over to welcome me with a kiss. I'm always a little shy around her. Uncle Zvalo, a body-builder, is grasping my hand so tightly it's unbearable; luckily, just as the bones are about to crack, he releases me.

"I can see that you've been getting into fights; you've got bruised hands. I'm telling you, you're going to grow into a real man real soon. Are you working out?"

"Yeah, I'm trying. A friend of mine is teaching me karate. He's a national-level champion."

Papa goes into the kitchen to get some coffee with Aunt Julia. Grandma has finished the dessert and continues the story she began before we arrived. When our Grandma starts telling a story, everybody stops talking to listen. She's glad to see me and Miky, and pauses her story-telling for a moment. We kiss her on her cheek and sit down on the carpet with the other kids. Grandma enjoys great respect as the head of the family.

She had been an important official in the Slovak government – not that I knew anything about that as a child – but there was something about her that still commanded

4

deference. "It was in 1943: a Nazi officer pulled me out of the wagon of that train and saved my life. I never understood why he rescued me, but I remember his eyes: he looked at me as if he'd known me forever. Somehow he was different from the other Nazis; I knew I could trust him."

"Grandma, what was it like in the camp? Could you go out for walks? What was the food like?"

"Lesana, dear, you know it was a long time ago and I don't remember it so well. After a war, you want to forget things like that."

"At school we learned that there were many guerrillas and soldiers in these camps. Did you meet any of them, Grandma?"

Aunt Julia now joins in:

"Of course there were many soldiers in the camps, but what kind? You remember, right? They were Soviet soldiers: the good guys. You know, you can use this at school: when Comrade Teacher asks, tell her that your grandmother was sent to the camp for being a communist."

"Wait, Julia – just hold on there – that's enough!" Grandma raises her voice and everybody falls silent – waiting for the explosion. Grandpa reaches out from the couch, and puts his hand on her knee in an effort to calm her down:

"Zdeňka, just let it be, please."

"No. I've had enough after all these years." She is crying.

"I have to tell you something. All of you, listen to me: I can't stand hearing any more about those wonderful Soviet heroes, the same army that came back to occupy us in '68. Of course some of them were heroes, and so many young boys died during the liberation. But the camps were not like what they taught you in school."

"Mom, what are you saying?" Uncle Milan protests.

"Milan, son, just sit down and listen." Grandpa comes to Grandma's aid. "You see, they want us to forget those who suffered the most: the Jews." "Jews? What Jews?" Milan looks warily at his mother, still scowling.

The room is suddenly very tense. Glancing around, no one seems to know what this is about, and many look like they don't want to know either. Grandma continues:

"The truth disappeared from the books many years ago. The old books have been replaced by new ones with pretty covers and safe words – the catchwords for our times, pleasing to the handful who govern this place. They want to ensure that they, and only they, are made to look like the victims and heroes of that era."

Aunt Janny, who a few weeks earlier had celebrated her graduation from a political college, is standing nervously by the doors to the balcony. She's the youngest of all my aunts and uncles. She's a zealous communist: already poised to become a leader of our bold new society – and she's listening in and shaking her head.

"Mom, what are you saying? The Jews were sent to Palestine and after the war they established Israel."

My father has been closely following the whole debate, drawing on a cigarette; now he interjects:

"Janny, respect your mother!"

"Let's see now: the oldest little brother, Mr. Big Communist, out of the blue turns against his own Party? Have you forgotten how the Party has helped you? What would you be in the broadcast without us?"

Papa mashes his half-smoked cigarette out into the overflowing ashtray and snaps back:

"Little sister: just listen to what our mother has to say for once! You've all been duped by the propaganda of this Soviet

6

'normalization' program." Aunt Janny is not so easily convinced:

"I'm not going to listen to this nonsense. There are kids here: you know, all they have to do is mention something at school and there'll be trouble – is that what you want? Is it?!"

Grandma is wiping away tears when her gaze falls on me:

"Did you know, he had eyes just like yours, Pauli?"

"Who, Grandma? Tell me."

"That officer who pulled me out of the wagon at the last moment, the Nazi officer."

"That's enough, Mom. There's nothing that can excuse the Nazis; they killed millions of people, for God's sake."

"Not all of them were evil; this one was good. If it were not for him, none of you would be here today, not one. He liked me – he was upset by what they did to me underground, when those pigs kidnapped us for their evening's entertainment. I was nineteen then but I've still got marks from my shoulder through my collarbone all the way up my neck"

She unbuttons her blouse and pulls it back on one side to reveal a slightly misshapen shoulder with broad scars running from the collarbones down up toward her neck. Even I recoil at the sight.

"Mom, that's just beyond the pale. Don't you think they're a little young for this?"

"Yes, that's enough," Aunt Julia joins in." This has gone too far. Pauli, Lesana, Miky, even you, Marcel: go play in the children's room, Grandma isn't feeling well."

"Aunt Julia," I ask calmly, "please let us stay."

I can see that Grandma would like to tell me something more.

"No, Grandma is drunk. Into the children's room, kids. Get moving, all of you."

She grabs me by my shoulders and pushes me in front of her. I follow Miky and my cousins out of the living room and into the long hallway leading to the front door. Just at that moment, Grandma jumps to her feet, and screams in her hysterical, shrill little voice:

"Because we're Jews! All of you, understand this: we are Jews, Jews! You, Janny. You, Paul. Julia, Milan: all of you are Jeeews."

It's hard to understand her; jaws? The kind with teeth? What sort of jaws does she mean? Is there something wrong with ours? My aunts shout her down, and the doors to the living room are slammed shut. Along with Aunt Julia and the other kids, I slowly drag myself into the children's room that had belonged to Uncle Milan when he was growing up. We can still hear the debate in the living room, which has become very heated, but I don't understand why there is so much anger in there. Grandma's piercing voice slowly fades as Aunt Julia closes the door. It is drowned out completely by the piano, which Auntie is using to distract us, the children of her new era. Something about this reminds me of the incomprehensible bulletin boards on the walls of our Communist Schools, where, several times a year, the teachers have us post projects from our art classes that have slogans we don't understand, such as:

"Children of the Communist Peace".

Grandma's memories are clearly not intended for children like us.

CHAPTER 2: JUST A FEW YEARS AGO, ON THE DARK SIDE

"So how many is it going to be, guys? Seven, eight, nine beers? I can't hear jack shit here over all your damned chanting."

"What'd the fat-ass say?"

"You'd better watch your mouth, innkeeper; if you're not with us, you're against us."

"He can't hear you; the noise is terrible in here."

"Look, here he comes."

"Paul, you'd better watch him. Hey, wake up man; you're, like, dead to the world. What are you daydreaming about all the time? The place is buzzing, beer is cold: come join in."

"Sieg Heil. Sieg Heil!"

From a small gym in a remote mountain village, Nazi slogans and songs spewing hatred towards Jews and other "low" races roll out in waves into the darkness. I'm sitting among their leaders up at Herr Heinz's VIP table, finishing my sixth coffee of the day. Every time I drift back from the past, I ask myself somewhere deep inside: what the hell am I doing here?

"Well that was something; what a ride! One day our time will come! Paul, buddy, you want me to sic an SD on you?" (That's a Sicherheitsdienst; a security detail.) "You're starting to look suspicious, dude!"

"Let him be, Dietrich, Paul is ours, I can vouch for him. This guy has proved himself. Unlike you – you're just sucking up to the big boys. Next time you accompany Herr Heinz to the toilet, make sure you personally inspect and then wipe off the seat before he sits down."

Proved myself? That was in the infamous attack on the Old-New Synagogue. I had doused the wall with gasoline and set it alight; the gas burned off in a second on the wet wall. But then we had the police night patrol on our back. They were no ordinary cops. They must have been athletes, judging by their speed in pursuing us. But as for us, after five blocks we ran out of steam...

We're standing in a dark alley in Prague's old town, all of us bent over, panting, and finishing off the packet of cigarettes before completing our glorious terrorist mission.
"They're here, Paul: you know what to do." Heinrich looks at me and nods.

"Freeze! In the name of the law, freeze!" I come out slowly towards the two frightened cops. Each man holds a telescopic metal baton in one hand and a tear gas canister in the other.
"I'm standing still; I'm not moving a muscle."

In two minutes we have to be out of here, the special unit will arrive any moment.
"D-d-don't move!"
"I'm not moving. We made a mistake, guys, you've got us. We'll

go back to the station with you and let you fill out a report. See, we won't make any trouble." He's putting the tear-gas back into its case and taking out his set of handcuffs.

"Cover for me, I'll cuff him."

"You two stay where you are. Not one move!"

"Sure, officer, we're not madmen, we don't want to cause any trouble." "What got into you, pouring gasoline on the wall of a synagogue? Don't you know you were recorded on security cameras? And you've got no escape plan, either, clearly. I can just easily shoot you, you know! Stay right there, where --"

"Ohhh...no."

"What the f...? In name of the laaa-w!"

And it's all over. They made a basic mistake separating from one another. But even if they hadn't, I'd have taken them down anyway. One attempts to put handcuffs on a two hundred-pound man, and the other, instead of covering for him, heads toward the rest of the detainees. It was so easy – you turn around, the cop takes one of your hands and before he puts on the first handcuff, you hit him with a rear-turn hammer-fist and knock him out with one good clean blow. If you happen to miss, you can still immediately come back at him with a good-quality quick hook – that's a long open hook with a clenched palm. Either way, he ends up on the ground. Then you kick him in the head or anywhere else you like. Next, you've got to take care of the other one before he gets his gun out. In a situation like this, only a professional can succeed – and that's a standard these patrolmen proved themselves not to be equal to.

"Jesus Christ, Paul, that was like goddamn James Bond movie. Let's get out of here!"

Heinrich comes back, kicks the prostrate, wheezing cop in the head with his heavy boot, and takes out his service gun.

"You're a damned Jew, aren't you, you snooper? You're a bloody Jew all right, a cop, a goddamn, fucking Jew." He aims the gun at the cop's head; the cop shrinks back, helpless.
"Fucking hell, Heinrich, let's get out of here!"

"You're lucky this time, Jew, 'cause we've gotta make haste, but you're gonna end up in a transport anyway."
"Come on, you hear those sirens?! They're coming from both sides: we've got to get out through the cellars. Quick, into the house. Move!"

So that was the glorious mission where I had proved myself, and that's why I can be here today, sitting in a gym in some godforsaken border town and drinking coffee with a group of modern elite SS members. Each one of them has a skull tattooed on the inner palm of his right hand, like the original SS men had on their caps. Each member also has to have a personal story that justifies his hatred towards the Jews. These people here are no ordinary skinheads; this is elite neo-Nazism, and they take it very personally. As do I. Nearly eight years have passed by, but the terrible events still feel like they happened yesterday. The memory is not only vivid, but every time it is reawakened it seems more real than so many other events. I haven't forgotten. Nor have I forgiven. Even in this unbearable cacophony, I can still see everything.

CHAPTER :3 IN THE US, MANY YEARS BEFORE MY ENTRY TO THE DARK SIDE

It's evening, a little before six. Emily has come back from a yoga lesson, and I'm watching television. She's in the bathroom, and the phone starts ringing. Andrea, an old friend and a former neighbor from Bratislava, is calling me. She says that Papa visited her. Apparently he looked like he'd been sleeping out in the rough, and he smelled awful. She gave him some warm soup and took him for a walk in the park. It seems that his girlfriend Magda has thrown him out of the house.

"He says he doesn't believe you're coming back, Paul. He's afraid ... he feels so lonely and abandoned. He told me a transit inspector threw him off a tram for being a vagabond and, as he was being dragged out, he passed by his sister Julia..."

"Julia, please help me. Can't you lend me even a little change...?"

"He told me that she didn't even look back; she just stared out the win- dow as if she didn't know him. He was crying as he talked ... Paul, are you really coming back for him?"

"Yes, definitely. There's still a month or two to go, but that's really the maximum ... They said that for young couples the immigration officers don't make any trouble. Please tell him I'm on my way, so he knows that everything's going to be all right. I'll come for him and we'll be together again in Prague ..."

My father is ill: he suffers from serious manic depression. When Grandma died, Papa was alone. The only thing he ever did for a living was write articles for a Bratislava newspaper and the Slovak broadcasting company, but a few years after the introduction of the market economy, and the arrival of democracy, he was let go. Maybe it was fate that shortly after Grandma's funeral, as soon as it was possible to leave the army, I returned to Slovakia, twelve years after I'd left.

I come home, bringing along a Czech accent that has become part of who I am. Of course I'm speaking Slovak here, but the locals immediately label me as a Czech trying to speak their language: a foreigner. I can feel the difference between the Czech and Slovak ways of thinking and know that I don't fit in like I did before, and won't be accepted the same way. I have been in the army since I was fourteen, but when I was finally able to leave, excited to go back to my homeland, it was only to find that I can't do anything there. I can't join the police force unless I serve for a year and a half in their army, but no thank you! I've had enough of that.

So I change careers and spend my free time taking my Papa to one psychiatric hospital after another. He is aware of his diagnosis and understands what it involves, but it brings us closer. Living together after those years, I finally come to know my own father. He is a pure soul, a man who never envies others and sincerely wants the best for everyone. Now that I am an adult, he shows me all the letters he tried to send us, returned by the post office every time. I finally get all the answers I'd sought so many years ago and I'm happy. We both are, bonding as only a father and son can. We cook together, pass long hours chatting on the balcony, go for walks, take little excursions, and visit hospitals and cafes, depending on the day and his condition. Always the intellectual, he doesn't handle practical chores so well, so I take over the cleaning and washing – but I refuse to iron. We earn our living writing brief articles. Papa is now making it as a freelance editor; his name is already known and his articles are usually well received. Half of them are written by me, so we split the money. We live modestly, but we are content. We visit aunts and cousins, but my childhood years are gone and now we all have our own stories and troubles. The ties have been torn. We know we are family, but there is such a distance between us now that we almost feel like strangers. Still, those two years in my homeland are wonderful, and they pass quickly.

Then, out of nowhere, a dispute arises over the ownership of a large house in the center of the city. The family falls apart squabbling over money, and there's nothing left of those fragile relationships that had worn so thin. It's only a mercy that Grandma and Grandpa can't see this. Papa's brother takes control of his share because it comes to light that bank notes are disappearing, handed out to the homeless, prostitutes, anybody who comes to my father with a sad life story. Unscrupulous people are playing on his sympathies for money and destroying his health, and it's clear that mine is going to give way too if this continues. I'm exhausted by having to drive all the greedy opportunists away.

The only one who seems like a little light in this darkness is Magda, Papa's girlfriend from the time when he had nothing but a typewriter and me. She offers help and I accept it out of despair. My intuition hints that something isn't right, but I keep ignoring it. I want to live my own life, and I have decided to leave again: to return to Prague or even farther – to the end of the world, if possible. I am saying my goodbyes with Papa in the living room over a pie Magda baked for us. Sipping at hot coffee, we promise to keep in touch. The sight of the new slippers he got for Christmas reassures me. He looks comfortable, and smiles as his new guardian tells me how strict and uncompromising she will be with him. No more night walks through the city and handing money to desperate people: from now on, he will stay on the straight and narrow. After the last sentence she strokes his cheek and kisses him. I pick up my backpack and, with a handshake, bid farewell to my father and to Bratislava, the city where my story began, where all of the heroes of my childhood are locked away within the wistful word "Once..."

"So tell him, please, that I'm coming. Feel free to lend him money, I'll pay everything back – you know I'm good for it. Above all give him that message, promise me you will ..."
"Well, when he shows up again, I'll tell him."

This call has made me very uneasy. The next day I call the INS's office in Chicago. They assure me that everything is moving along smoothly, that the last interview went better than expected, and that it was in the interests of all concerned to avoid having a lawyer present at the next one. All I have to do is abide by the law and not leave the USA. The female clerk noted that they were sorry about my father's situation, but...

All we can do is wait. Papa will be fine, he has to. He'll visit an old friend, stay with him for a few nights until that old witch Magda finally relents and lets him come back to her. Most likely he was making noise after ten in the evening, or disobeying her rules again by hanging around cafes in the city. It's going to be all right.

Another month has passed. Work today was really good: I'm driving a bus like a pro already. During my break, I went to a training session at Fay's gym, and the people there were checking out my speed and endurance: I'm getting very fast – and built, too. I feel great. My wife Emily and I discuss our upcoming trip to Prague. She's looking forward to it a lot. I tell her stories of my childhood and she corrects my grammar. I'm making fewer and fewer mistakes in my English now, but this is still helpful. We go to the cinema almost every Sunday; it's become a habit. Before the movie we go to a cafe or drop by the Häagen-Dazs shop. I get a huge milkshake with ice cream called "Dulce de Leche". The people around us are all students, judging by their clothing. They seem to be enjoying their independence for the first time, though their behavior shows they've got a long way to go before they will be ready to be truly independent from their families. But what business is it of mine?

And so the weeks go by. I'm home watching a video we rented from Blockbuster. It's evening and Emily is just back from her yoga lesson. She's started cooking. She's taught me a few really good recipes; her tortilla stuffed with minced meat, cheese, and chili peppers seriously releases my endorphins, especially after a long day of work and training. This is just another carefree and relaxing evening, but why is the phone ringing again?

It's probably Vlado or Laugher, calling to remind me about the party on Saturday with the Czech au-pair girls. I don't know if I'll go. Emily is keen to meet my friends and practice her Czech, which she's been studying for a few months now. She's making good progress too ... But at the other end of the phone, it's not Laugher or Vlado – it's Andrea calling from Bra- tislava again.

"Paul, you've got to do something – your father's been out on the streets."

"Please, just tell him what I told you."

"You don't get it, Paul. Magda's cleaned him out – she's taken everything. She's withdrawn the rest of money your father inherited from his brother in Nitra. She told him it was for you, that you needed the money. Then she sold the apartment, which she had renovated with your father's money, and left. Nobody knows where she moved. Your father has nowhere to stay and he's broke. Paul, for God's sake, if only you could see him. When are you coming, for the love of God?"

"Shit. Shit. Damn it! Jesus Christ!"

"Paul, your father's sleeping on a bench in the city. He's completely homeless, and he's not in his right mind. No one knows where he is, and no one's taking care of him. Do you get that? Are you there?"

"I'm coming very, very soon, two or three weeks at most. Give him money for food; he can stay with "Shepherd". You know, the guy who used to put him up for a couple of nights whenever he got Magda mad. That damned witch."

"You know nothing: Shepherd's an asshole. He beat your father up several times and threw him out of the house because he smelled so bad. Your father was in floods of tears when he told me all this. I'm desperate to help, but I don't know how. My father doesn't want him at our place, not even for meals, because he makes the kitchen stink. And I can't give him money either; I also live from paycheck to paycheck. He still thinks of you all the time. You're his only hope!"

"Okay, here's what you'll have to do ... Go downtown, to the Prior shopping center. Ask the tramps when they last saw him and where he usually sleeps. Find him and take him to the Salvation Army, they must be somewhere in Bratislava. Find him, you hear? Tomorrow I'll send you $500, that's almost 25,000 Slovak crowns. You'll book him a room in a cheap hotel for two weeks, okay? Tell him that every other day you'll give him five hundred crowns for food and cigarettes; if he gets any more, he'll just give it away, you know how he is."

"Paul. Where should I look for him? You think I have time for this?"

"Just listen! I'll give you $300 just to find him and take him to the fucking hotel... I'm coming back very soon, but in the meantime it's up to you. Are you listening?! I can't leave until I get a green card! Otherwise they won't let me back into the country again, understand? Then everything will be fine. I'll split my time between Chicago and Bratislava, a few months at a time. I'll have money and I'll get Papa his papers to come over here... everything will work out great if we just get through the next few weeks. Will you do that for me ...?"

"Well ...when will you send the money?"

"Tomorrow I'll wire it to your account; I think it takes three days to go through. Promise me you'll find him and rescue him ..."

"Well, I'll try. But, Paul, please come soon, he's only got a lousy summer raincoat on him and he's cold – it's the beginning of winter already ... Seriously, can't you come any earlier?"

"He'll have to hang on a few weeks longer. I can't walk away from everything I've been building here. This place is a paradise. If you could only see it ... if you work hard you can have a house, clothes, vacations, whatever you want; I can train with martial arts masters; perhaps I'll even raise my children here someday. He'll love it here. He'll find a new woman and begin to live happily again. We'll be together, and you can come and visit us with your little girl."

"You know what – forget about that. Just come back and look after your father. Take care – and send the money at once!"

"What happened?" Emily asks me, but I don't feel like talking. My father has turned into a grimy beggar. How could I have trusted Magda? Only because it was convenient at the time. Inside, I knew that she was a self-serving bitch. It was a comfortable lie. I reproach myself: just admit that you didn't want him at home in Prague.

I continue berating myself until I finally fall asleep. The next morning is even harder than the night before. Do I really want my father with me? Here in America? And is Andrea really going to use the money the way I told her? She often lies and she's known to be a bit lazy: she might just pretend that she couldn't find him, but then remember that she had to buy a few things for her daughter. I know her: she's going to wait until he knocks on her door again, then maybe she'll give him something. But is he going to knock? She told him that he can't come around, because of her father's delicate nose.

Am I being selfish? Yeah. Shamefully so. So how about giving up on the damned green card and going back to help your father, huh boy? No, no way. He's got to hold on, he can handle it ... After all, I can't give all of this up; at home I'd be scraping along to make a living like everyone else there. What kind of a life could I build for us there? It would only be survival, but if I can get my papers here it'll be the ticket to a better quality of life for both of us.

"If the issuing of this card could be sped up in any way, I'd be truly grateful. I recognize that some people might make up this kind of story as an excuse, but I'm telling the truth. My father is in a precarious situation and he needs help. I'll go home as soon as I have the card in my hands."

I'm nervous. This is my last interview with the immigration officer. Then all that remains is to wait for the notification letter. Emily is sitting next to me, holding my hand. We look like a couple in love, there shouldn't be a problem. But she squeezes my hand when I mention Papa. I don't get it, it can't influence anything; on the contrary, I think. The balding man leaning back in his comfortable armchair looks me up and down, considering my case. It's clear to me that he's no ordinary officer. These higher-ups call themselves immigration officers because they give the final approval. They can refuse to issue a green card without any explanation, and just send a letter with a deadline for leaving the United States as a last farewell.

That won't happen in our case, though. We're a young couple and we look like we're in love; or at least Emily does. I know she wishes our marriage were genuine: we get on so well, we talk for hours, we treat each other with kindness and patience. Maybe this is what a marriage should look like.

"Yes, yes. I follow you, and of course I believe you. Don't be worried, you won't have any problems. If only you knew the cases that come to us. Most of the time it's a fat, elderly divorcee with a young Mexican. Of course, they never persuade me, especially when she cannot speak a word of Spanish and he can barely string together basic phrases in English. My father is also in poorish health, so I understand your predicament; hopefully he'll be all right. We've found a beautiful place for him in Florida in a Jewish community. It's really nice there, and he's settled in happily. In a few days the whole family is flying down to celebrate my fourth son's Bar mitzvah with him."

"Excuse me? Sorry, I didn't understand."

"Sorry, it's not English. In Hebrew it means to welcome a man spiritually into the community as an adult. It's a very important tradition."

Emily joins in the conversation: "Yes, I thought so right. This is Jewish, isn't it?" She points to the mantelpiece. "That's a menorah. And you're wearing a kippah."

"Yes, that's right, you know your stuff! Is someone in your family Jewish?" "Jesus Christ, I hope not, ha ha ha." For God's sake, why couldn't she have kept her mouth shut! Too late. Everybody has gone quiet in the room. "Sorry, I didn't mean it like that."

"Very well then," the immigration officer cuts in, "we'll let you know soon. Enjoy the rest of the day and good luck. Goodbye." He gets up and quickly shows us out of the office. I don't have a good feeling about this at all. We shouldn't have gotten into a discussion about Judaism, we should've just kept our mouths shut. On the way home, the silence in the car is deafening.

"I am so sorry, Paul."

"It's okay, he was an understanding man; hopefully it'll be all right. Don't worry, Emily, this can't influence anything."

Two weeks flew by in no time but there was still no notification letter. In the meantime, Emily has made progress with her Czech; her pronunciation is breathtakingly good. I like her more and more. I'm starting to think, what it is that a man seeks in marriage? Is passion really so essential? We had tried making love several times while drunk, but every time it was a fiasco. We both laughed about it afterwards, but I heard Emily crying in the bathroom after one of our attempts. She wanted this to work – so badly – and I feel deeply obliged to her. I'll fulfil our agreement to the last by helping her get established as a painter in Prague, a city of artists. I know so many people she has to meet; surely they'll love her and help with everything. But damn! If only that letter would hurry up.

Another fourteen days pass.

Today, I struggle to get out of bed in the morning. I've taken a job on the cargo ships. Last night we were on the river putting a giant tanker together: five barges wide and seven long. Two other units were called in to help us. I've never done a more exhausting day's work. It was like working out for twelve hours straight. You're constantly screaming as you're pushing or pulling a heavy load of iron, and then there's the never-ending tightening of the wire lines. On the other hand, I've never felt more manly than at I did the end of that shift.

I'm going to make some coffee and check the mailbox. I feel that today is going to be a special day. No, the coffee can wait – I'll check the mail first. I walk past the fridge, where Emily leaves her sticky notes with messages. Before leaving for work this morning, she wrote:

"It is coming soon, Paul :)" She's a nice girl. Please let it come today. Imagine you've got a lottery scratch card, and as you scratch off the last box you reveal the symbol for a million dollars. That's what it was like for me to open the letter.

"Dear Mr. Batel, we are pleased to inform you that your permanent residence card has been issued and is ready to be picked up at immigration Schliesmann's office."
Yes, yes, yes, I've done it! I'm going home, Papa, soon everything's going to change, very soon.

"So here you are again, Mr. Batel. How is your wife? Is she looking forward to going to Europe? You're taking her with you, aren't you?"

"Of course I am. She's looking forward to meeting my father. "
"I admit, Paul, I did have some doubts about your case; something did not seem right."

"Wait, what do you mean?"
"Well, after a two-week delay, I said yes. You see your green card has been lying here for nearly three weeks. Some things just take more time." "Excuse me, but you've had it here for three weeks, even though you know that my father..."
"Oh please, everyone claims that their mother or father is in trouble, and asks to have it sooner..."
"But I wasn't lying ... I ..."
"Well, here it is, so off you go. And remember, in two years we will meet here again."

So for three weeks he's had it lying on his desk; what a sly Jew! But who cares, I've got it and I don't give a damn about anything else. I'm out of here; I'm going straight to the library to book a flight on their internet-enabled computers. Finally, finally, finally! Then I'll head over to the Cup Foods market to buy a couple of bottles of champagne. Emily and I will be celebrating tonight! I'll ask her to make sushi. I'd never eaten sushi before I met her, but when she saw how I loved it she taught me how to make it and it's become something we enjoy on our best days.

"Hey: show me. I'd like to see it; is it really green?"
"Nah. it's silver, it just has a greenish strip on the back – look here." "Wow. I'm really looking forward to going to Europe."
"I'll open a bottle now, huh?"
"Okay."
"This is for our journey. You'll love my Papa; he's a wonderful man. I've learned so many things from him. Oh, I've told you that a million times, I'm sorry."
"Don't be, I can't wait to meet a person who's influenced you

so much. Why do you call him "Papa "? In Czech it's "Dad," isn't it?"

"Papa" is Slovak. I've called him that ever since I was able to speak. I used to see him for only two weeks every year, and calling him "Papa" separated him from my Czech dad. That's what I had to call my stepfather."

"I've made sushi, since you like it so much."

"You know I was going to ask you to do that today? You're amazing, Emily, really amazing."

"I'm also your wife." We both burst out laughing. I laugh so hard I start crying. We are both so happy.

But destiny is spinning its own web. In the middle of our giddy private celebration, the phone begins to ring. I pick up the receiver laughing and with a smile on my face, something I will become incapable of for the next two years. By now it's been nearly eight years since I answered the phone that night in Chicago, and I'm still unable to recount the details of the call with my brother from beginning to end without my shaking chin making me close my mouth.

An extreme frost struck Slovakia unexpectedly early that year, at the beginning of November. A record eight homeless people were reported dead on the evening news.

One of them, was my dear Papa.

CHAPTER 4: BACK AMONG THE DARK ONES

"Hey, Paul. Paul!?"

"What?"

"There's something going on here. That fat innkeeper is getting a beating, dude. I told that fricking Jew to shut his face; he was too full of it."

I'm back. At least for fifteen minutes I didn't hear a single voice despite the noise in here. In the meantime, Herr Heinz has returned back from the stage, accompanied by Kurt, and bedlam has broken out in the tap-room. The innkeeper didn't get that he should have just stuck to running his business and kept his fat mouth shut. Or he understands exactly who he dealing with. It's not very easy to rent a place for these purposes and keep it a secret, and sometimes it's too much for the hosts and hired staff to bear.

Things aren't going to end well for the innkeeper, but I've become worried about the waitresses, his good-looking daughters. They're trying to hold back the skinheads, who are furiously kicking every part of the innkeeper's ample torso.

And now the skinheads have got hold of them and are already beginning to tear off their clothes.

I look at Herr Heinz who is watching everything with interest from the VIP table. I hesitate for a moment; I don't want him to think I'm losing my nerve. I can feel his gaze shift from what is quickly shaping up into a gang rape scene down there back to me.

"Interesting how this turned out. The officers have taken a liking to these girls; maybe they even have a claim to them. What do you think, Paul?" "I was expecting elite soldiers, Herr Heinz; these men have no discipline or distinction. I await your orders, sir."

"Excellent. You're absolutely right; this behavior is unbecoming of officers. Take charge here and show them who's boss!" I am relieved. I don't need to hear any more.

"Heinrich, get up, I need a hand. Tell Wilhelm to park the cars behind the house and come with me. Dietrich and Franz, stay with Herr Heinz. Kurt, you come with us as well – what are you staring at? That's an order from the Führer, so move it!"

We're ready. We're standing at the back of the small crowd that is throwing around the two now naked waitresses, who are in shock. They resist the groping with all their strength, crying hysterically, pleading, and trying to cover their modesty. I'm waiting for Heinrich.

Finally, he puts down the phone, which is a signal for me that the cars are driving around the building to the rear entrance.

"Now!"

We tear a path through the crowd of officers from the hallway to the kitchen. Heinrich shouts to the desperate girls:

"Run this way, goddamn it!"

Finally, they notice our narrow escape route and run through. Kurt is running with them. He shows them the way and tells them to trust him. "Now!"

I sprint out of the crowd with Heinrich just as the path we have forged through the enraged SS men collapses. We're trying to catch up with Kurt and the girls, who are now running through the kitchen, across the yard, and through the back gate into one of the waiting cars. At least a dozen skinheads in heavy boots are chasing us; it took them a while to decide to pursue their stolen prey, but now they are after us. The back doors of the black BMW saloon are open. The frightened girls don't need to be persuaded to get in; Kurt slams the doors after them.

"Go now. GO!"

Wilhelm steps on the gas. He's taking the girls to safety, to a villa where Herr Heinz resides. Heinrich turns around to face the pack of neo-Nazis that has just reached us, and pulls up his sleeve.

All of them stop. They know what his tattooed symbols mean and to whom they belong. Heinrich's other hand is grasping a Luger P.08, an original gun used by a high SS officer. I am one of Heinrich's favorite guards, part of an elite group that he has chosen himself; but I must admit I hadn't expected this from him. He reacted very quickly; he won't relinquish his authority.

Heinrich Eichmann is one of the great nephews of Adolf Eichmann. He used to be a personal guard for the leader of the most powerful neo-Nazi organization in Western Europe, and he's responsible for dozens of terrorist attacks on Jewish community centers, synagogues, and schools.

Needless to say, he is one of the most wanted criminals in Europe. He has been living in Prague for a few months now.

31

He organizes meetings for Herr Heinz and celebrations in remote villages and gyms all over Europe. Everybody falls silent. They line up and raise their right hands to greet their legendary leader, and then shout in unison: "Sieg Heil!" The message has spread throughout the gym and the line formed by the skinheads leads back to the stage. We slowly return to the innkeeper.

"How is he looking, Paul?" I lean towards the battered body. They have kicked him to death.

"He's finished."

"Issue the orders to the men to dispose of him. Take the body away and dissolve it."

"What's going to happen to his daughters?"

Heinrich looks at me and with a contemptuous smile walks towards the stage. He climbs the stairs, stands in the middle and with a short speech introduces one of the five most influential neo-Nazi leaders in central Europe.

Herr Heinz takes the stage to rapturous applause. He waits for Heinrich to sit back at our VIP table then, with his arms folded on his chest, looks around the teeming but mesmerized hall. Two minutes elapse before Herr Heinz breaks the silence. His words play well with Heinrich, who stands up and, filling the whole room with his hoarse voice, shouts:

"Sieg Heil, mein Führer. Sieg Heil!"

The neo-Nazis gleefully respond:

"Sieg Heil! Sieg Heil! Sieg Heil! "

The subject of Herr Heinz's discourse that evening was the unification of the neo-Nazi elite across all of Europe: Greece, Germany, Russia, Poland, Hungary, Slovakia, Austria, Italy, Spain, and of course the Czech Republic. He discusses preparations for this secret pan-European reunion and for the election of one leader. The whole spectacle, with constant heiling and fanatical speeches, drags out till morning. For the rest of the night, the men pour their own beers, and the innkeeper is forgotten.

I drive Herr Heinz home with Heinrich and Kurt. Dietrich and Franz follow us in an armored van belonging to a certain security agency, which helps cover up the real identity of the convoy. In the car everybody speaks German; they have no idea I understand at least half of what they're saying. Heinz says he likes me and asks Heinrich for his opinion. He answers that I handled today's intervention well, even though he could tell how sorry I was for those girls.

Heinz is worried that I might be too sensitive for tougher events. Heinrich tells him that he thinks it will be necessary to leave me out of the assaults on Jewish children being planned in Stuttgart and Warsaw. At this, Herr Heinz burst out laughing and asks:

"What do we need him for then?"

"He's a trained liquidation machine," Heinrich replies, "and Jews killed his father ... Er ist unser Mann." Heinz stops laughing and replies:

"Ja, er ist unser Mann." This point of accord – "he's our man" – is satisfactory for the time being and, as of next week, I'll receive a pay rise. We park at the villa, where I hand over the car keys to Wilhelm, who closes the electronic gate behind us with a remote control. Together they head for the villa and I to my parked car by the fence. Heinrich turns to me one more time:

"I'll call you. I have a good deal for you next week, a really good deal: look forward to it."

I couldn't just leave things there.

"What's going to happen with those girls?"

"Sometimes you ask too many questions, Paul. Keep that in

mind."

A few weeks later I find out from Wilhelm on the way to Frankfurt that the innkeeper's daughters were sold to one of the German roadside brothels as prostitutes. But before that, back at Herr Heinz's villa, his men had doped them up on heroin and raped them for several days until they got bored of them.

Maybe I should have left them to the drunken neo-Nazis. What would have been better for them? To be raped to death, fully conscious, by a hundred animals at their father's inn? Or to die of a heroin overdose, feeling nothing at all in a cut-rate whorehouse?

I can't seem to shake this off. Compassion. I have come to hate the world around me with all my heart, the system whereby the corrupt decide the destiny of ordinary people who get up at half past five every morning to do an honest day's work. A world where how much money you have determines if you are a respectable man or not, where connections are more important than talent, where nobody gives a damn what you really feel. Where, without the mask of confidence, people attack you like predators and don't let go until you put the mask back on.

This world deserves the terror and chaos these madmen wreak; what do I have against them? I need money to survive in this wretched world and take care of those I secretly care about.

I wanted to be a proper man who answers only to himself; maybe I used to be him. But at some point he was overwhelmed by a stronger force. I don't know where it suddenly appeared from, but I know its names: envy and malice.

Fate had dealt many unkind blows, but I'd never wished to

end up like this, not really. Somehow a monster had been born from a sensitive and fragile boy who used to recite poetry. When did this start? And where? Show me, destiny, or whatever they call you. God? I want to go back, right now.

Come with me for a while. Yes, you, come and watch a young boy's journey from innocence to becoming a skinhead beast. In the end, the past will become my future. My destiny, my curse. And my calling.

I long to be that small, fragile boy once again and know nothing of this.

CHAPTER 5: IN THE WOMB OF DESTINY

It's a beautiful morning and the smell of freshly cut grass is wafting through kindergarten when the teacher shouts: "Everyone inside, time for lunch!"

I can still picture the lady by the fence giving me a little badge with a boat on it. She said she was from Russia and (speaking only Russian) called me krasivyy mal'chik (beautiful boy), telling me I had a bol'shaya (great) future. She was kind and pretty, and it seemed just as if a fairy godmother had stepped into my life.

The teacher orders us into the room where the toys are kept, magical toys that come to life at night, and asks if any of us can recite poetry. "Maybe you, Kristina?" Kristina begins but her voice is halting and the teacher isn't satisfied with her performance.

"That was nice. How about you, Tommy?"
Suddenly two other teachers come in with a strange lady who isn't wearing plastic covers on her shoes like everyone else. For

some reason this time the teachers and the cleaning lady don't mind. It's that nice lady from the other side of the fence. She looks around the class and smiles when she sees me. "Zdes, etot mal'chik." (Here, this boy.) The teacher calls on me to recite a poem. I can't think of one off the top of my head. I am conscious of an uncomfortable tension; I have no idea that it's called stress. The mysterious stranger is a bit disappointed, and the teacher calls on little Evi instead. She's shy and, in a quiet voice, mumbles something about a frog. Meanwhile, I'm racking my brains: come on, think of a poem, you know a few after all. The foreign lady, although she's listening to Evi, is still looking at me. She notices the smile on my face when I finally remember a poem about a guerrilla and encourages me: "Pável vspómnil na básničku. Pável, daváj." So she speaks a little Slovak too. Everyone enjoys my recitation, and the nice lady is clapping as if I've taken a weight off her mind. She has found a suitable boy and thus fulfilled her mission. Why, I don't yet know.

A few days later, I'm walking onstage accompanied only by the same nice lady who is leading me by the hand up to the microphone. In front of me, maybe a thousand people are sitting in suits and ties. I feel uncomfortable and, in a soft voice, start reciting a poem about a guerrilla who doesn't get frightened in the valley of shadows. About a warrior who, hurt and abandoned, throws himself under enemy tanks holding a grenade. He has no regrets about his destiny. He doesn't feel sorry for himself even for a moment. With only one line to go, I stop. I don't even know why. I am immersed in the poem, my heart is beating hard, my chest rising and falling in the white shirt buttoned up to my neck. Time is standing still. I look around the great hall, exhale, and finish:

"Yes. He has fallen for peace, for his brothers and my

homeland!"

A five year old boy has just finished reciting a poem about the guerrilla he would like to be like one day, a story of heroism and sacrifice which he treats with a grown-up seriousness. After seconds of stony silence comes the explosion of applause from a hall of trade unionists, now all on their feet. I notice a figure forcing his way down one of the rows to the aisle and heading straight towards me. I can't believe who it is. My dear Papa, coming up to the stage and shouting:

"That's my son! That's my son!"

"Pauli, what are you doing here? I didn't know you'd be here. Look, the whole crowd is cheering for you. It was perfect! I'm so proud of you." Everything is spinning, I'm being led backstage.

I don't know how I got home. I don't recall if we returned to kindergarten with the teacher, or my Mom, who picked me up that day, only Papa, with his wide-eyed happy face, and then the applause and the noise. What a coincidence, my dear Papa.

That day something changed. I can't say what exactly, but I started to be considered special by the grown-ups: neighbors, teachers, older children, even people on the street. I remember perceiving it – and agreeing with them that yes, I was special. However, I didn't know that it was because my recital had been recorded at the annual convention of the Central Committee of the Communist Party of Slovakia in the presence of the top political leaders and broadcast on the main evening news. I had no idea that the children's symbol of progressive socialism for the year 1980 was me.

CHAPTER 6: AFTER RETURNING FROM HOSPITAL... A FEW MINUTES BEFORE THE BIG MOVE

"We can finish our swords with those large pieces of styrofoam we found yesterday by the fence."
Peter likes the idea; he's happy that I'm finally out of the hospital and back with my family and neighborhood. We pierce square pieces and create dueling cords of a kind. We've already had the blades ready: narrow branches of elder wood, sharpened with the tiny fish-shaped knives that all children seemed to have in those days. Peter and Miky test their cords in the first light duel and find that the styrofoam protects their hands on the grip. It was a good idea to use it for this, and Peter and my brother are appreciative.

"Wow, it's working."
Miky suddenly hears Mom's voice. "Pauli... Miky!" "Mom's calling," Miky says, putting the sword back in the pile of improvised weapons. We're on the lawn in front of Peter's

house, just around the corner from ours. "Peter, you hold on to the swords; we'll play with them again tomorrow, agreed?"

"Okay. Why do you have to go home so early?"

"No idea. Maybe there's cartoons on TV – we told Mom to call us if some- thing good came on ..."

"After that, we'll come out again, I guess," I chime in.

"All right. See you later, then."

We run around the corner of Peter's house and head through the park straight to our house. In front of the apartment building there's a huge car. A few big guys, along with one of our neighbors, are carrying furniture out of the building and putting it in the back of the car. Mom's waiting outside the front door; she says we have to change quickly. We go upstairs to the apartment, and find it almost empty.

"Come on, come on." Mom says, helping me take off my muddy sweatpants. The nice man who's lived with us for over a year, the one who's happy when we call him "Dad," takes the last armchair from the bare living room and walks past us as though he doesn't notice that we're there. "We're moving." Mom says, as she forces the sweatpants into a backpack crammed with stuff. Miky and I are stunned into silence. Too shocked to protest, we follow Mom into the car she indicates, where a driver is already waiting. Outside, neighbors and children have gathered to send us off.

The car starts to move and everyone is waving. Miky and I wave back. We're going on a long journey in search of an adventure. Miky suddenly notices Peter, as we turn the corner and pass his house. He's sitting on the front steps adjusting the styrofoam on our new swords. We both wave to him, but he doesn't notice us. We realize that this afternoon he's going to ring on our doorbell and there'll be no one to answer. We pass the blocks of high-rise apartment buildings that for eight years, or nine in Miky's case, have marked the border of our neighborhood. A border we had never crossed, or even wanted to. In our district we had been safe. In our district, we'd been at home.

CHAPTER 7: PRAGUE

"K Sídlišti 398: this is our new address," Mom says enthusiastically as she helps us unpack. "We're going to like it here. Wait until we go out, you'll see! Look at all this green space – and we're right on the edge of Prague. Feel how fresh the air is here."

"And if we don't like it here, we'll go back, right?"

"You bet. But we will like it here, don't worry. "

"Come on boys, go help unload the truck. It's all up to us here," Dad says, throwing down a carpet he has just dragged up the stairs to the third floor, where we now live. My brother and I help him lift a large wardrobe out of the car. I can feel how heavy it is and I don't see how he can expect us to carry it up to the apartment.

"Don't you dare drop it! There's expensive stuff inside." We stagger up the stairs; neither of us knows why Dad is so angry when we stop to catch our breath on the first floor – after all, it weighs over two hundred pounds.

It's almost midnight by the time we go to bed, sore and exhausted. Miky and I lie awake talking for a while, wondering what Peter, Lacko and Drahuška might be doing. Then reality hits us, and we start crying. When are we going to see them again? And what about Papa? On Friday, he was supposed to pick us up. When are we going to see him? We didn't say goodbye to anybody. Why didn't they tell us? Overcome by worries and memories, we eventually fall asleep.

"Well, gentlemen, get up," Dad bursts into the room, "it must be seven o'clock already!" He throws open the window: "It smells like a pigsty in here. In the morning you'll help put this place to rights. Then, after lunch, it'll be time to study. I already have Czech textbooks for you."

"But Dad, it's summer break," Miky protests confidently.
"I'll give you a break," and the man who just yesterday had been such a nice gentleman slaps Miky across the face. "That's for being cheeky."

I'll never forget Miky's surprised expression. It was the first time he had ever been hit that hard. My big brother starts crying and I comfort him. The 280lb giant rushes back into the room.

"Here's another, so you know why you're crying!" He starts beating Miky savagely all over his body. I throw myself at his arms in an attempt to stop the powerful punches. The hysterical crying and screaming wakes up Mom and our little brother, who's a year and a half old. Mom comes running into the room and Dad stops punching immediately.

"What are you doing, for God's sake?"

"Oh, please, they were being rude. They don't feel like studying, because apparently it's summer break."
"Boys, what's the matter with you? Cut it out." Miky and I are huddled together and neither of us can stop crying. Miky's

choking and panting for breath. Mom comforts us and explains that we have to obey Dad.

"From now on, things are going to be different for you, gentlemen," we hear from the kitchen. "In September, when you go to school, you'll be able to speak fluent Czech, and you'll know the material they're teaching at least three months in advance. Is that clear?" We get up to change into sweatpants, still quietly whimpering. "Above all, you must not cry. There is nothing I hate more than that."

Several days later, we meet Tereza, who lives next door and is the same age as us. She shows us around the neighborhood. I admit that it's really nice here. Somehow we cannot truly appreciate it with Miky along, but I have other concerns. Now my brother and I get a beating every day. Mom sometimes intervenes to stop her huge beard-man. But often she agrees with him that we need to be punished – because it is good for us to be disciplined. "Come on, don't take it so hard. Dad only wants the best for you." Quietly we ask her if it is possible to go back home. Mom tells us there's nowhere to go back to.

A new phase of our lives has begun: there is no turning back now. Our stepfather storms into the room yet again; his heavy footsteps signifying that he has just discovered something he isn't happy with. Maybe poorly washed dishes, or unsatisfactory vacuuming. He wants to test me on my schoolwork in the living room. "What do you call this?" Bam, whack, smack. "After this movie, I'll test you again and God help you if you don't know it then! Miky, I'm gonna test you too, you better count on it!"

Miky is sitting at the table and, instead of studying, is staring out the window. I know what's going on in his head, where his thoughts are. I'm there with you, bro. But now we're here, and in an hour we have to know this stuff cold, or else...

That evening, I pass my stepfather's test and am allowed to watch a cartoon before bed. Miky isn't so lucky. He hasn't learned anything. The beard-man beats him so badly that it is a while before he can walk again. Mom is out on an evening stroll with our little brother and can't intervene. Not really a coincidence, but rather part of a new pattern. I hide under the covers, I am awfully scared. Miky calls to me for help – and then he stops.

In September, we have our first day at our new school. I'm looking for class 3B. The building is huge, much bigger than our school in Bratislava. The teacher introduces us to the class and we take our places in the third row by the door. The class is discussing the months of the year and their characteristics:

"This month is September. After September comes – why don't you tell us, Milan?"

Miky gets up and says that his name is Milovan, which means "Beloved." This provokes raucous laughter among the children, who begin taunting him: "whom do you love, Milovan?" We get the feeling that this place isn't very friendly. The teacher snaps at the class to calm down. I'd like to help Miky, but I don't know how to say "Oktober" in Czech. I tell the teacher that we don't know Czech well enough yet.

"But I heard that you moved here early this summer. You live in the Czech Republic now, so it would be good to learn to speak Czech."

"In Slovak, you say Oktober," I remark with pride. With pride in my language: the only thing we have left here, apart from the memories of our friends, Papa, Grandma and Grandpa. The ones who were always so nice to us. In Bratislava our teacher used to smile when she tested us. This elderly lady has a harsh voice and looks very strict.

"Sit," I hear, "or bring me your Pupil's Book."

During the break, my brother and I sit at our desks and look at each other. Fear is mixed with determination to handle this. Our classmates are staring at us. Some of them ask us questions: "what's it like in the Slovak Republic?" And, "where did you say you were from, from Bratislava?" And, "which place is better? Do you like it here?" They keep staring.

"Yes, I do. Here we can climb the trees, we couldn't do that in Bratislava." I can't think of anything else to say. I want to please the locals and perhaps even make friends.

We are still blissfully unaware of what a note in the Pupil's Book means: we don't know that this is how Czech teachers communicate their dissatisfaction with pupils to their parents.

Our stepfather sees the revelation of our ignorance of the Czech names for months as the worst sort of disaster. That night he beats us for what seemed like an eternity: "September, October, November, December. This disgrace will not be repeated! I'll thrash it into you!"

Two battered puppies curl up under the table; their mother is out for an evening walk with the stroller again. This is starting to resemble hell. How many more beatings are there going to be? Maybe we'll get the hang of Stepfather's requirements soon, and then they'll stop. Miky's not doing a good job of learning Czech. The beard-man sits with him and repeats the names of the months again and again: "June, July, August."

Something begins to change in Miky. He apathetically gazes out the window. He ignores Stepfather, who again and again beats his nine-year old body that is already covered in bruises.

The days begin to pass quickly, as they do when every day and week is the same. On the street I notice the looks by children and people who pass by every morning on the way to school. They talk about us and sometimes even rudely point at us. In the classroom, some of the straight-A-type girls stop greeting us, then others follow suit. From other classmates, we learn that the whole street hears the screaming from our flat.

One night, when Mom sends me out to empty the garbage can, I find clusters of people standing around outside. They're looking up at our window and on their faces I can see wide smiles. Then they notice me and move a bit further away. We are their evening's entertainment, but they have nothing to say to us.

This is how immigrants become known as weirdos.

The days and months are flying by. Stepfather has introduced a new rule to be observed during the beatings: we mustn't cry because we'll wake up our little brother Jarry. When this happens, instead of using his hands Stepfather reaches for the thickest wooden spoon in the kitchen – and only now do we understand what pain is. And crying doesn't stop it.

On the street, on the way home from school, older guys start to shout at us: "Slovaks! Hey Slovak, what're you staring at?" We try to ignore it, but the boys won't give up:

"Fucking Slovaks!"

Although Miky begs me not to, I turn round and shout back:

"And you're fucking Czechs!"

Then a group of five or more surround me. Sometimes they leave Miky in peace. He curls on the ground and hugs his school bag for comfort. This is my fight, guys. I don't feel punches and kicks. They are nothing compared to the daily pain dealt by the giant beard-man at home. I try to hit at least one of them and return his punches, but fail to do so. Fair fights in Bratislava, where a crowd would stand and watch boys fight one-on-one, are now just a distant memory. And it does no good to be attached to it, as my brother already knows. Actually, it seems to me that Miky escapes more and more time into his dreams, so much so that he's not here anymore.

A few slaps are waiting for me from Stepfather for my tattered shirt. But for the grade of 'D' I got on my Czech dictation exam, it'll be a slaughterhouse. I'm starting to think about what it'd be like if Mom had never met this beard-man from Prague. And I'm also thinking about how differently Stepfather behaved when he lived with us in Bratislava. I remember his outbursts of anger, which he would quickly contain and for which he would later apologize for hours. My gut told me then that there was something wrong with him, that he was hiding a lot more, and that intuition was right on. I often look up at the clouds, and I ask them, "Tell me how to turn back the hands of time."

Finally, our first year in the Czech Republic ends and summer vacation is about to begin. Last day in school. Miky doesn't feel like going home with two 'D's, in Czech language and math. I have two 'C's, in the same subjects. We walk slowly. I comfort Miky, saying he doesn't need to worry. Stepfather has known about these grades for a few weeks already, so he won't thrash him. Miky wipes the glasses that he's been wearing for a couple of months – studying late at night by the light of the bedside lamp has weakened his eyesight. He starts to cry:

"I want to go back to Papa and Grandma so badly. You don't know how much I think about it, every minute, every second. I don't belong here. I can't stay here any longer!" I'd like to soothe him, but have no clue how, and at the same time I'm increasingly worried that I'll be the one who'll get the worst of it, because I was expected to get only one 'C' and I'm bringing home two of them.

To hell with it, vacation is starting and Stepfather won't be back from work until four o'clock. The day will pass peacefully at home with Mom. She'll let us go out and play in the woods.

There I feel good.

But: we get home and Stepfather welcomes us. "Don't worry guys, I won't bite. It was a tough year, but we managed. Well look, just two 'D's. If I didn't test you every evening, you would have had 'D's in everything!" Then he turns to me:" Well, Paul, what is it? Two 'C's?"

"I'll study over the holidays, Dad, and next year I'll make up for it. Really." "I know. You're a hard worker – unlike Milovan."

Someone's ringing the doorbell. Mom welcomes a rare visitor. Prague Grandmother, as Miky and I refer to her, has come to see us. I can feel something in the air: something's not right. Something's very different today, and soon I find out what's afoot.

Miky has dreamed so much about freedom, few can imagine how hard he has wished for it, and now his wish has finally been fulfilled. I'd say that its fulfilment has come just in the nick of time. I don't know how long he'd have made it here. Even though we lived together in one small room, we were becoming estranged by my success at school, for which I was allowed to go out in the evenings as a reward, while Miky had to sit by the window and study. He was also getting pounded twice, even three times a day. I usually got just one daily beating. We were together almost all the time, but inside he felt alone.

"Milovan's going to live with his father and grandmother in Bratislava and you, Paul; you're going to stay here with us. It'll be better for everyone this way. The two of us get on better, after all, and I'll make a proper man out of you, you'll see. I'll have much more time for you when Milovan is gone. "

"I'm going to Papa?" Tears begin to flow down Miky's face. He removes his glasses and tries to wipe them away with a used handkerchief. But these are tears of joy for finally being sprung from this prison. Is it possible that when we wish for something so wholeheartedly and strongly it has to come true? It seems so. But what about me? What's going to happen to me? When can I go back to Bratislava?

And so I get it: I had been trying so hard to learn to please the beard-man, to be the best I could be, that I have completely forgotten what life was like before we came here. I have forgotten to remember my loved ones back in Slovakia. When the memories came flooding back, I immediately tried to forbid myself from thinking about them, and over time I became more successful at not remembering.

But Miky had never given up. The fighting heart of a Leo, the sign under which he was born, had never faltered. Never, not even for a second, did he leave his true home. Now he's saying goodbye to me, embracing me with a smile:

"I'll see you again, bro, you'll see. Don't be sad..." He takes his suitcase, which Mom has already packed for him, and embarks on his happy journey back to "paradise".

I remember that I was standing in the living room by the window and waving to him. The same way I used to wave to my dear Papa before he disappeared around the corner, after he'd returned us to Mom on a Sunday. My step-grandmother then grabbed me by my shoulders and asked me a strange question:

"Are you sorry that your brother's leaving, Pauli?"

In life, there are only a couple of occasions where you can say: "I'll never forget what I said." This was the very first one

and I have never felt such intense emotion again ever:
"I envy him terribly, Grandma, I envy him so much."

CHAPTER 8: TWO YEARS LATER

"If you want another sugar cube, Pauli, don't be shy. I'm willing to give you one more."

"No thank you, Grandma, one's enough for me." We're visiting Prague Grandmother. I'm sitting at a table, sipping tea. The beard-man nervously smokes one cigarette after another. Today's a big day.

After two years away Miky's coming back here on vacation to see Mom and me. I don't know if I can say that he's coming to see our half-brother Jarry too. He wasn't even three years old when Miky left and they never had a chance to play together. Miky rarely went out with us because he wasn't allowed to leave his textbooks and his desk. By now I've actually gotten used to him not being around just like I've got used to everything else in this foreign country. But the memories of all the years together are still strong, so I'm looking forward to seeing him so much. Any moment he and Mom are going to show up in the doorway.

"Please, Ivan, control yourself. Don't scare the boy the moment he steps through the door. You know how steamed up you get sometimes." They're whispering in the corner of the balcony overlooking Prague's Olšany cemeteries. What a heartless hag she's become. I once liked her. I believed that she was an ally who would stand up for me. But not so long ago I overheard her talking to the beard-man in the kitchen at home, claiming that I furiously attacked her demanding fifty crowns, and that she had no choice but to give me the money. Outside, I was caught that day by some older guys. I didn't know them and was expecting a whipping as usual, but these guys, even though they knew I was a Slovak, didn't beat me up. They wanted me to join a soccer team – they were missing one player. They took me with them onto the field and their coach greeted me pleasantly. He said that in order to play I had to bring fifty crowns for insurance and registration fees. I ran home as fast as I could, happy that this was the first time they wanted me to join them, and not to beat me up. Excitedly, I asked this Prague hag who was babysitting me and little Jarry for fifty crowns. I told her what it was for; she looked knowingly, and without hesitation gave it to me.

The truth hurts, someone once said. And what we perception may be quite different than reality. The wicked old nanny-goat looks at me smiling and speaking kindly. Sometimes she even strokes my hair and tells me that I'm a perfectly brought-up young man, and father's strict upbringing really shows through. And then she quietly makes a repeat offender out of me, even though she knows what will follow when she leaves. Stepfather hastily bestowed a few slaps upon me, but it was the shouting that was unbearable. I stopped going to the soccer games anyway. Every time I lost the ball, they swore at me for being a Slovak. Once I was dropped in the middle of a match because the coach joined them in a fit of anger.

I don't need this, I told myself. What's the name of this irrational rage? Nationalism?

The doorbell interrupts the quiet discussion in Grandmother's Žižkov (Prague's district number 3) apartment. My gaze is fixed on the entrance. What does he look like now? Mother looks excited.

"So here we are. Well, Milovan, come on in! Take off your shoes and greet your dad. Do you remember Grandma?" I know that he doesn't give a damn about them. Do they think he's forgotten the sleepless nights hunched over his textbooks, or the icy showers followed by thrashings when the beard-man caught him asleep on his desk at midnight?

"So, Milovan, welcome back to Prague. Oh come on in, don't worry, please. What are you standing there for?" Stepfather's deep voice is scaring him. Miky is standing in the doorway and through thick glasses he surveys everyone in the room, wide-eyed. His gaze alights upon me, and he smiles faintly. Finally, he starts taking off his shoes. I get up from the table and walk over to him. The old hag bars my way. I have to join the queue; my elders take precedence. "Welcome, Milovan. The two of us don't know each other very well, but that is going to change. I'll come and visit you more often now, and help your dad with your teaching. I've bought two 'Parisian desserts' for you. You must be starving after the long journey, right?"

Miky doesn't pick up on this little detail, but I do: she just said that she'd help Dad with teaching him, and that means what...?

Finally, it's my turn to greet my brother. We stand facing each other and for a while we just look at one another. Both of us are smiling. We shake hands.

"Hey bro. How've you been?" He greets me in Slovak.

"Okay. I've missed you. How are Papa, and Grandma and Grandpa? " "They all send their love, and they're looking forward to seeing you ..."

"Wait a moment, Milovan. Let's get this straight right at the start: now you're in the Czech Republic so you have to speak Czech! Is that clear?" Miky continues to look at me in silence and he's smiling. As if he didn't hear the beard-man. "Your cousins say hello too. All of them send their love," he continues undisturbed.

"Is he kidding? Does he think he can just ignore me?" Stepfather is more than annoyed; he, Mom, and Grandmother move out to the balcony. "Please don't be so fierce, honey. Wait until he's finished eating dessert to correct him. After all he's just arrived, and needs a while to collect himself."

"Grandma's right, Ivan. Let him breathe now," Mom adds.
"You see what his father and that witch have done to him in Slovakia? It'll knock them on their lazy asses when they see what I can make out of him! He'll learn to respect his elders and not act as if he didn't hear them talking to him, starting right now!"

"Calm down, Ivan, let it be." Mom and Grandma manage to placate him for a while. "Come on, Milovan, sit at the table. I'll give you dessert. Do you remember me at all, dear? I'm your step-grandmother. Pauli, please help him with his suitcase."

Miky finishes his Parisian chocolate cake with whipped cream. Mom quietly encourages him to share it with Stepfather to initiate a reconciliation. Miky knows that Stepfather has heard Mum's advice, but he wants to please her, so he politely asks Stepfather, in broken Czech, if he wants the some of his "welcome" cake.

"Oh, please, you wouldn't have offered it to me if your Mom hadn't told you to."

"No, you would have offered it anyway, wouldn't you Milovan?" Mom's trying hard to keep the peace.

"Yes, of course I would."

"Okay. You know I'll take it. You see, you're a nice guy, Milovan. I've always had good intentions for you. We have a little surprise for you. Your mom and I have been following your progress at school for the last two years and we have to tell you that we're horrified. Several 'D's on your report card? That's terrible! They certainly let you do whatever you want over there. Nobody is guiding your study, and this is the result."

I still don't get where the beard-man is heading with this. Miky listens to Stepfather and nods, but he still doesn't understand what's happening. "... and so your Mom and I have decided to keep you here and make a smart boy out of you." Mom immediately joins in to lessen the shock. "Well, Miky, you don't want to grow up to waste your life sweeping the streets somewhere, do you?"

They simply won't let him go home! That's what he was whispering about with the old hag!

Miky is silent. He stares at the floor. Slowly he's coming to realize what it all means for him. I stare at him, wondering what to say. On the one hand, I'm happy that my brother will be here with me again but, on the other, I'm terribly sorry for him. His wish, once fulfilled, has just been snuffed out. I know how good they are to us in Bratislava. And I know, like Miky, what it's going to be like here.

"But Grandma and Papa will be waiting for me," protests Miky weakly. He's already accepted his fate. He was looking forward to the holidays and seeing his mother and brothers for two weeks. He would never have come if he'd known what to expect. And so Fate has, once again, woven its own web and changed one small life.

He was brave, so it took a long time before the lively and cheerful boy with the heart of a Leo was, thanks to his stepfather's screaming and ceaseless beatings, finally ... broken.

CHAPTER 9: FROM THE DARKNESS, I VISIT MY BROTHER

"Today we made this, well ... for you," he takes a dark green cube-shaped molded candle from his large coat pocket.

"Thanks, Miky, that's very nice, really. I'll find a good spot for it. I think I'll place it in the center of the table. You know that little glass table in front of the TV? It'll look good there." He lights another cigarette and calmly looks straight ahead.

"Give me one too, Miky. I'll have one with you."

I've been visiting my brother here for several years. I try to come every day because I don't want him to feel alone. Sometimes it doesn't work out, like when I have a contract and I'm often away for several days. Miky usually feels worse when I'm away and doesn't go out on walks with his group. He just lies staring at the ceiling. But he is always overjoyed when the nurse calls out his name: "Milovan, you have a visitor! Your brother's here."

We're smoking and looking at the autumn leaves. There's

a huge chestnut park here. The trees surround the high-rise buildings within the walls of this institution for the mentally ill. Miky lives in one of them. Perhaps I'd be better off hiding myself away here too. I tell him about work. Miky has a favorite story about how I ran away with a client from one restaurant on the outskirts of London, when instead of the Nigerian diplomats he had an appointment to meet with, a bunch of hulking gangsters arrived.

The "infamous London job"

I'd known from the beginning there was something fishy about this, and tried to explain to my client that business meetings don't usually work this way. I warned him of the danger – that they'd threaten him, and that the briefcase full of cash would be the only thing they'd want. He didn't listen to me and, instead of cancelling this contract, I went to the agreed place – against every bodyguard's cardinal rule. Like anyone else might have, I was hoping I had been wrong about the risk, but more importantly, I needed the money. Twenty grand is twenty grand, after all. It was lucky that there was another grim little pub right across the street from the one where the meeting was to take place ...

I seat him next to a window and tell him to watch who's coming in. I go through the kitchen looking or a back entrance for staff. It is there, so I am relieved. The alley at the back, full of garbage, leads, in fifty yards, to a main street where London's black cabs are whizzing by.

I return to my arrogant intellectual client and sit down with him at the table. I light a cigarette and we wait. We've arrived quite early. I'm counting on the fact that no one is expecting us in the pub opposite. No one is. At the desk, he tells me how paranoid I am, that I'm not cut out for this kind of work. He'll pay my fee, of course, but the next time he'll definitely select another agency, and make sure they send him someone who's more professional and doesn't get on his nerves. I keep silent and stare out the window at the pub across the road. Maybe the idiot is right, I am jumpy.

But diplomats, even when conducting private business, just don't meet in neighborhoods like this.

Ten minutes later, two cars arrive. Half a dozen huge Africans leap out and run into the pub across the street.

"I'm sure those aren't our guys, they'll come later. I'll call them." He still doesn't believe me.

Before he can call the number, the strongmen run out with the bartender, who points at us through the window. My savant turns off his phone and looks at me, astonished. He wants to say something, but the words don't come out. Quickly I get up and shout at him: "Let's get out of here! Come on, get up! Do you hear? Shit, man, get up!" No reaction. I drag him to his feet and, using a wrestling move, throw him over my shoulder. Fortunately, he isn't heavy. I kick open the swing door to the kitchen and, running through the back door, enter the dirty back alley, and from there to the main street. It is only fifty meters away. I've run about twenty when I hear the thugs yelling behind us. No time to look back. Over my shoulder, my terrified client is struggling for breath. He wants to say something, but he can't. I make out something like:

"Behi ... behi ... beh—."

He wants to say that they were behind us. That much I know. I feel like throwing away the briefcase full of cash, and maybe the useless weight on my shoulders too. I run right into the middle of the main road. A couple of cars swerve to miss me, sounding their horns. I drop my cargo on the ground: "You've gotta run now. Go!" So we run. My legs are shaking; I can barely stand on them. A flush of adrenaline causes your physical condition, however fit you are, to decline by at least eighty percent. Twenty remains. And that twenty percent disappears faster than you can say "Nigerians". We run in the opposite direction down the road. My guardian angel is with me, as always – thank you, Papa! Just as our pursuers reach the road, I stop a black cab and bundle the egghead inside. I jump in after him and shout, "Go!" The driver steps on the gas, and as we pull away I manage to get a look at my pursuers. Years of jungle warfare had done terrible things to the faces their mothers gave them. Those scarred mugs definitely look like they belong to killers.

I finish telling my London story, and Miky, as always, seems rapt. He sits back and smiles, smoking another cigarette from his endless supply. They are the only thing he buys at the institution's snack bar.

"Remember when we were playing in front of the house with Peter?" He asks.

"I remember, Miky. Do you think about our childhood often?"

For the rest of my visit Miky doesn't say another word. I have to go: I have work in the evening. They want to know if they can trust me. I'm going into action with Heinrich. I don't know the details, but something's going to happen tonight in the Jewish Quarter.

"See you soon, Miky. Relax and think about our next trip. We'll go somewhere, like a castle. Stroll up the hill. We'll have an espresso and a cigarette somewhere with a nice view."

CHAPTER 10: BEFORE ENTERING THE DARKNESS

Four and a half years have passed since I returned from Chicago. Memories of America and Emily have long since faded into the past; contracts for protection are all I am concerned with now. I've worked in several night clubs as a bouncer, and had several shorter-term romantic relationships. And from the shortest of all of these I now have my little princess-Maria.

Trying to live with a stripper was foolish. When you're working as a bouncer in luxury strip clubs, you have to expect that sooner or later one of the ladies will take an interest in getting to know you more intimately. Many of them have experienced trauma and yearn for a protector, someone with whom they can feel safe. But when you try to keep your distance it only entices them to try and charm their way through your defenses. In their work they play the role of beautiful hunted beasts, but sometimes they also like to be the ones on the chase. You need a good deal of tolerance to live with one of them; but the same is true of living with one of us. Working as a bodyguard you are expected to travel a lot, you get unexpected phone calls in the middle of the night, and then you have to get up and disappear. You might be missing for two or three days, sometimes even a week if, for instance, you're escorting a client to a meeting in Bosnia. I believed that if I was tolerant towards the strippers' lifestyle, they'd tolerate mine. Tolerance for tolerance – doesn't that make sense? To me it does. Because what these fancy girls have to face in their relationships is that sooner or later their boyfriends or fiancés begin to reproach them for what they do.

I didn't. I tried to understand them. I was watching them at work and realized that they lead a double life. On stage and then during the private dances they wear a mask to attract and hypnotize men, taking advantage of their egotism and naiveté. Many men believe that when a beautiful woman smiles, snuggles up to him and, with a look of a passionate desire, slowly undresses for him, it's because he's the strong and successful man she longs for. He's got no idea that the woman really loathes him and inside is laughing to herself, saying, "you can't buy me, you poor man ... two minutes more and I'll forget what you looked like ... You're dying to sleep with me? You're dying to meet me tomorrow for dinner? But of course ... I'll promise you anything, just slip some more currency into my thing ... the night's long and you think you'll have a chance to try and seize me. But at 5am I'm gone, and if you don't come tomorrow and try to win me again, you can go to hell!"

And this is also the way it goes when you live with a stripper. It soon becomes clear that you're going get no tolerance: they want to have total control of the life you have together and own everything that's yours. The lady wants to go out, and not just anywhere. What if you're working? "Then just take a day off when I do!" It's not possible? Finally, it turns out that the mask she wears at work is no mask at all. "What? You want to leave me? You, you scum of the earth, you hand-to-mouth destitute?" A last farewell party ... we can still be friends, right? ... That's when, after two weeks, I come to pick my last few shirts and shorts that I'd left there.

Why not? A little relaxation tonight can't hurt, and the promise of a massage? There's just one little thing she forgot to mention: she'd neglected to take her contraceptive pill ...

One massage, one last night ... a few glasses of chilled champagne ... and nine months later Maria comes into the world. A little princess, a new being who's clearly destined for great things. In your head, you hear the words of your father: "Pauli, now the moment's come when you need to act like a man. You know men don't leave a woman alone in distress ..."

"I'll do my duty, Papa, don't you worry ... I'll do my duty."

She knows I won't leave her; she knows I won't have anybody else. After a few months, we rent a new apartment. She knows I'll stay a while after the baby's born, until she returns to work. Two strangers sharing an apartment is hard; we bicker over little things and try not to let it escalate into fights. But trying to walk away from a newborn little miracle is even harder. If only her mother could change a bit, or at least try to change: if she softened a little she could learn not to despise ordinary people, not to judge them, and not to humiliate them – particularly when she's the one who hurts others the most.

At least, that's how I saw it in those days.

So I leave. I rent an apartment and take care of little Maria while her mother goes to undress for her customers. And so I have her with me four times a week. I accept fewer protection contracts and, in my free evenings, I teach members of special units and bodyguards how to fight. Twelve-month-old Maria cries and fights with all her strength when I take her back to her mother in the morning, leaving her with the nanny while her mom sleeps after the night shift. It tears my heart apart and reminds me of my own childhood. Perhaps we could try to be together. There are probably more important things than my own comfort, peace, and ego. Her mother says "yes", and I meet her conditions – a large luxury apartment in a nice neighborhood, and my savings are wiped out.

Trying to coexist like this with Lucia becomes increasingly unbearable. She doesn't try to restrain herself from making poisonous remarks when she realizes that we're really together "just" because of little princess we call "Maru". I call her also "Bubu". The quarrels are endless. She does whatever she can to provoke me, and I find it more and more difficult to control myself. The little one scuttles between us in the middle of the shouting and doesn't know who to hug first to make it stop. It's much worse now than it was before. I have to go away forever and accept that Maru, as she grows up and starts her exploration of the world, won't have her father by her side every day.

And so a few more years pass.

Due to the economic crisis, there are fewer contracts; officers from the fighting units are dismissed, so my trainees disappear. There's less and less work, and more and more gangs of striplings and crooks in the streets. The news talks about neo-Nazi groups expanding and their organized attacks multiplying – even though many are foiled and their perpetrators caught.

Today I'm going to pick up Maria. Her mother calls me to tell me that I can't come until five o'clock. Alois (her upmarket new boyfriend) is looking after her, but her mother insists on preparing the little one personally. Huh ... perhaps Alois could handle that; why should I wait until five and waste half the day? Today I'd like to take Maru to the zoo! Miky's got a job there, sitting all day in a shed and drawing. I'm glad at least something could be found for him. We'll visit him and then we'll go look at tigers. Yes, Alois can handle it ... I'm going to get Maru right away. I get lucky: a neighbor lets me into the building. I've met him a few times, so he just nods his head when I say I'm going to the fifth floor to collect my daughter. Screw the elevator. I like to go up the stairs. I'm tramp up to the fifth floor, when I hear a scream coming from one of the apartments. I start to feel a chill as I slowly approach Alois's door, because that's where shouting is coming from.

"I told you that you clean the room before I get out of the bathroom ... You had half an hour for that. You're not gonna make a fool out me, do you hear?"

"Oh... Nooo! ... That hurts! Please ... I'll clean it... reeeally! "

"Come and look at this mess. I won't just stand idly by while you do what you like. Stand up and stop crying, I'm telling you ... Get up! No? All right, I'll make you get up! "
" Ouch ... Nooo ...! "

My brain instantly short-circuits, and I can't control it in any way. I hear Maria running to the door, where he catches her and starts walloping her. She screams again and he throws her onto the floor and drags her by the leg into her room. Not even ten locks would keep me from kicking down the door! It

72

flies open immediately; I'm standing in the doorway to the children's room and it's quiet. The stepfather gazes at me in shock, and so does my tearful little girl. I am wearing the expression of a murderer who's determined to kill. Control yourself, please ... fight it ... come on ... I'm begging you please ... I hear voices in my head. And time stops again.

I'm with the master in his home gym in the suburbs of Chicago. We're back from the local tournament that I just won. Now we sit drinking tea at his round table at the end of our very last lesson. The next day I'm going home ... with Emily to Europe ... to Prague.

"You say that in Europe you're going to continue to fight? No, my friend, that's not the purpose of martial arts. One of the principles is to return ourselves to the present moment. It doesn't make any sense? With the support of extreme training you rid yourself of all fear. Once you get rid of fear, you can finally begin to perceive things without it. I'm talking about spontaneity ... about freedom of expression. You can finally be what you really are. Not what others expect you to be. You obey them out of fear – they're all around you, all of society is based on them. Understand ... the fact that you won today is a good thing. Take the best out of this. You've done it. You wanted to ... you were afraid of it and then with toil and effort you overcame it. I'm glad I could help you. Competition, however, isn't the real purpose of martial arts: the goal is to ultimately master yourself. The longing for that sweet feeling of victory over and over again – your craving to be admired and respected – is a prison. The desire of your ego, my friend, which only detracts from the beauty of this moment ... You'll begin to move away from it again. Finally, you'll lose one bout, then another... Then you'll have a lot of work to do to let it go. Do you know how much energy it'll cost you? You'll be somewhere else, rather than in the here and now. Thoughts will fly around in your head, your reactions to challenges will be dictated by your surroundings. Eventually you'll be forced to live only among people who have the same problems, with the same uncertainty of being, that you have. And that's a destructive spiral. To jump out of it then will be much more difficult than it is now: now's the moment, my friend, right now. Now you already know how to control your ego and thus also your inner anger. You have no idea just how lucky you are. Don't make any unnecessary steps back."

"Daddy!" Maria runs to me and hugs me tightly round my knees. We leave quickly, taking just her jacket and shoes. A few hours later Lucia turns up at my place, with the police. We're in the middle of making pancakes for dinner. Little princess greets her mother as if nothing has happened.

"Maru, Mom's gonna take you home now, okay?"

"Mom, why are the policemen here?"

I know that now I cannot do anything. I tell her we'll see each other soon. I manage to hug her. She feels the tension: she knows that something is going on.

"Mom, I'd rather stay with Daddy today. You know, I definitely want to stay with Daddy." She's my baby doll. But how can I explain this to her? The cops are silent, waiting for Mom to take away her daughter. But I can see the regret in their eyes. Alternately we all look at each other.

"No, Mom's gonna take you now, you're going to sleep at home. I forgot to tell you – tomorrow morning we're leaving..."

"And where are we going, Mom?"

"Well, we're going to see Aunt Simona and Tereza – I totally forgot about it ... Dad forgot to tell you too ... "

"Yeah ... Maru... I completely forgot... Never mind, we'll see each other soon, as soon as you get back, okay?"

What a trusting little soul this beautiful girl is... The tension eases. She loosens her grip and lets Mom put on her jacket and hat.

"Can I take a pancake for the road, Dad?"

"Sure. Wait, I'll put it in a plastic bag for you. "

"Why are all the policemen here, Mom?"

"They're your Dad's friends. They came to tell him something... " "Dad, are they your friends?"

"Yeah, that's right, Bubu, they're my friends. Run along with your mother, now, go ..." Lucia slowly takes Maria away and I feel that this is not going to be good. She turns to me, waving. She looks at my face and sees it full of concern.

"Mom, you know what? Come and get me in the morning when we go to Aunt Simona, all right ...?" She breaks away and runs back to me. She clings to my knees again ... She didn't buy any of our play acting ...that's my small, smart Bubu ...

Lucia begins to shout. I kneel down to hug Maru one last time, whispering to her that she really has to go, that everything is okay. Lucia is tearing her from my arms, and I don't want to betray my little girl and just let her go. She realizes quite well what's going on, and starts screaming and crying. "Dad, I wanna stay with you ... pleeease ..." She sniffles on the shoulder of my jacket. I hold her and try to convince everyone that I'll bring her the next morning. One of the cops hands me a court order and announces that starting today, and lasting until the trial, I can't come within three hundred meters of Maria. She begs me not to let go of her. And I don't want to, so badly! Finally, however, I release her ... I tell her not to worry. But I know I'm also betraying her...

I didn't want to make any trouble; I knew that obstructing the court's decision could lead to criminal charges, and that would mean losing my license to own and carry a gun, which is a necessity for my career. I had no idea that they had already filed a criminal complaint against me for kicking down the door. They've got breaking and entering, illegal restraint, kidnapping, and threats as charges against me. Lucia and Alois' plan worked out, they took her away from me ... Now they're taking away my gun too, along with the license... How am I supposed to work now? When am I going to see Maru again? Hatred starts to glue the shreds my life together. It's the only thing that has enough strength right now to do that.

"Mr. Batel, you are aware that your behavior was violent and absolutely unacceptable in front of your little daughter?" I look around the courtroom, viewing the Thomason family's excursion group almost everyone is here ... In the third row, Maria's sitting next to her Aunt Roza, who is constantly whispering something to her, and she's waving at me.

"Dad, Hiyaa!" What kind of mother takes a small child to court to hear about how violent her father is? That clearly doesn't make any sense. All she's likely to remember is that Dad was that bad guy who had to be sentenced by a judge.

I look at Judge Kaufman; she discreetly smiles at one of the witnesses sitting at the side of the room: Thomason, Aunt Roza's husband. Lucia's employer, the owner of the fancy strip joint, is sitting right in the center ... the rottenest lardass in town! What's going on here? They all know each other? But this judge he seems so cozy with can't be her ... the one the club owner told me about that day in the garden, back when I was taking care of Lucia while she was pregnant. He mentioned an influential Jew who helped him arrange his club's license and delivered bribes directly to the Mayor of Prague...

This just cannot be "the" famous Judge Kaufman!??

Lucia testifies about my use of drugs. For instance, after Maria returned from visiting me she found a bag of weed in the little girl's pocket ... She believed me when I said I'd quit, but the ladies and gentlemen in the courtroom have to understand that I really didn't ... every time she sees me, she feels that I'm under the influence of marijuana. The truth is that once a week I smoke up, but never in front of the little one. One evening, Maru was looking for the remote control to the television; I was in the kitchen getting her dinner ready. She reached into the drawer and found it. And unfortunately she also found a silver bag, which she hid in her pocket. It was a big mess. Lucia yelled at me over the phone for about half an hour, which she had every right to. I should've kept my stash somewhere else entirely, I admit. One learns through mistakes, right? Now everyone says that my aggressive reaction, kicking down the door, was associated with drug addiction. They suggest a drug test on the spot, in the courtroom, as evidence that I'm constantly under the influence. I never kept it a secret that I smoke – once a week, sometimes maybe twice, but rarely.

"So, Mr. Batel, do you agree with the test for the presence of addictive substances?" It's a good trap ... they know that weed can be detected up to ten days after consumption.

"No, I do not. I never smoke when I have my child with me. I light up after a difficult week, on Friday. Some people go to the pub and get drunk, I sit in a chair and take a couple of puffs. You're trying to prove that I'm an addict, but that's ridiculous!"

They dig up my abusive childhood and the related mental

disturbance. They say that Alois only reprimanded Maru, disciplined her, because she has learned bad habits from me. She doesn't obey and acts up a lot, because I let her do whatever she wants, and he and her mother have to their work cut out to cure her of my bad influence.

The court's sentence reads: I will be allowed to spend three hours with little Maria on the first Monday of every month. Violation will result in a complete ban until the next court date, two years later.

I lose my temper. I start to shout at Kaufman. "You just can't do that to us! What kind of a dirty trick is this? She and I are used to each other; we see each other three times a week ... you have no right to do this!"

"Calm down or you will be fined for disturbing the peace and for contempt of court. You'll have a chance in a couple of years to prove that you are worthy to take care of a small child ... after receiving drug treatment and finding a stable job. The case is closed."

"You're one corrupt Jewish bitch! How much did Thomason give you for this, huh? Do you think I don't know about that?"

Court security comes to restrain me, they want to take me outside. I can hear Maria starting to cry; all of them try to comfort her, then rise quickly and usher her out of the court.

"You should be ashamed, Paul, scaring your child like that." This remark from Aunt Roza peps me up. With a simple lever I force one guard to his knees, I want to kick him, but manage to stop myself in time. Another two come to help and a clerk calls for reinforcements. In the crowd, I notice the Thomason family leaving the courtroom with Maru. The second cop holds out a steel nightstick and the other pulls out an electric stun gun. The deep-rooted reflexes are stronger than the necessity of sometimes allowing oneself to be beaten – with no witnesses, in the now empty courtroom. I grit my teeth again, the survival instinct has kicked in – and then I hear them again, from a distance, in my head, the words of my Pa-pa. He's talking to me in a gentle voice from the other side:

"This can be handled another way. Wake up and use your brain! You can't hurt them. If you try, you'll never get to see Maru again. If you go to prison, your daughter will slowly forget who you are, and memories of how you played and hugged each other will be erased by new experiences over the years. So stop it. Stop it right now!"

And so the cop's nightstick lands, smashing into my collarbone. And a stun gun shakes all my ribs. My knees give way and I protect my head with clenched fists. I scream as if I'm being tortured, when the electricity now coming from both sides causes all my muscles to spasm.

"You cop bastards ... Kaufman, you Jewish bitch!"

"Come ON, you really can't," I humbly plead, in a conciliatory voice, at the door.

"I've told you plainly – on Monday the third you come for her, you won't see her sooner."

"But that's still fourteen days away. I miss her."

"I've told you to get out!"

"How can you be such a bitch?"

I squeeze my hand into a fist. I feel like crying, but I'm keeping it together. I'm not going to get through to Lucia like that. All the training and tough experiences are nothing all of a sudden, when it comes to a little girl you love purely and honestly. I'm completely hopeless and she knows that. "You're starting to be aggressive again. This discussion has just ended.

And if you don't leave right now, I'll call the police. Then you'll be placed under house arrest – you realize that, don't you? Get out, junkie, if you don't want to make my day. I won't have my daughter in the company of a psychopath and an addict any more than necessary. The court has made its decision. See you on the third – and only for three hours!"

"That Jewish beast; I hate her as much as I hate you."

She slams the door and the situation ends, returning to its stalemate; I can do nothing more. The bitch is right: if she calls the cops they'll write a report about me threatening her and God knows what else.

They've taken my little Maria away from me. For the past five years, I've been used to seeing her often. She would stay in my apartment overnight three times a week. I even sacrificed three relationships for this commitment, because apparently some childless young women have a strange, hidden aversion towards a boyfriend's children. Especially when they realize that the guy they have their eye on plans to spend time with his child more often than every other weekend, which is the most typical arrangement in this country. Three times a week is beyond their limits of tolerance. Well, they can go to hell too! My little one is everything I have. This one pure soul is the only good I can see in this disgusting world now. There were once other dreams, but where have they all gone?

One fateful day her mother discovered a bag of marijuana in her pocket along with a stuffed toy and a pair of scissors. Maru's a clever little vixen, I shouldn't have let her look for the damned remote control. She likes to search for interesting things in the drawers. I'm not angry with her because I also liked to explore in drawers and closets. There's nothing more fun for a child than to find, say, a stapler and staple some sheets of paper together herself. What does it matter that the paper is daddy's passport? What's that, anyway? I had to laugh that time: who would have punished her?

Kaufman, and what was the name of that immigration officer – Rosenheim? I forget. If he hadn't kept my green card in the drawer – just to savor his own power over a desperate immigrant – for two more weeks, my dad would have been here with me. None of what I'm dealing with now would ever have happened. We would have been taking walks with the stroller, he'd have seen his granddaughter grow up. He was looking forward to being a grandfather so much. Her uncle Miky would've been just fine, too.

Forgive me, Papa. I'm fed up and I'm not going to be such a sweetie-pie anymore. That guy died with you now.

Should I have used a lawyer at the trial? Saved money? Money! But I'll get that somehow, and I'll come back.

CHAPTER 11: MEETING WITH DESTINY

As Destiny wove its web, a tattooed man discovered me not long ago, while I was sitting in a wretched pub in the outer districts of Prague. I was wandering aimlessly through the streets, kicking trash cans and sometimes even cars. I was waiting for someone to confront me – someone on a balcony, with a little bit of courage. Then I'd throw a nice rock right into his mug. Or at least into his window; but what if I miss? That night I didn't soil my filter of hatred. Or did I?

I'm sitting in a putrid dive bar and drinking another warmish, revolting-tasting beer. I'm trying to figure out the point of my existence, just like everybody else. I'm thinking that it would be best to somehow seize the present moment, my ticket to a better mood and a cleaner way of thinking. Just the way it's written about in books, or as my combat teacher in

Chicago explained that one day, too long ago. I don't have anything to hold on to in this moment, though. Certainly not the foul brew sloshing around in my half-liter glass. The claptrap that elevates you when you're already cool, all that crap about the Tao, an ever-turning circle, opposing forces mingling with each other has deserted me: here it's just a bunch of sad guys all slowly poisoning ourselves in a fog of smoke, over how many beers? I've lost count.

"Bring me two more, would you?"

Contracts are hard to come by now for a skinhead without a weapon. Requests for private lessons in martial arts are coming in less and less frequently, and even money for food is running short.

I often watch my Maru from behind a fence, hiding like an old pervert in the bushes or hunched between parked cars. Around ten o'clock the teacher lets the kids play in the schoolyard and they start running around shouting on the monkey bars. Finally, I see her, my little one. She has no idea that her daddy is watching her; she's too busy with her dolly. She has her own child, in a beautiful world, with a list of chores she needs to complete at kindergarten before she goes home.

Sometimes I sit in the bushes, breathing in the vapors of piss left there by dogs and bums, but somehow I don't mind – because for a blessed short while I can see my princess. This is the happiest time of my whole day: I become someone different, and for this hour I can see the world painted with her colorful crayons. I picture a tiny house and a garden in a park where we play. We are fooling about and scuffling, I'm teaching her how to shake off someone who's holding her from behind. I teach her. I watch her crawling through a wooden castle with her friends, and recording the scene in my mind.

I'll think of something; I'll get you back. We'll have everything. I wonder if you'll ever remember me, Maru...?

"Life's a bitch sometimes, huh?"

"Excuse me...?"

"I can smell your rage from across the pub, mate. And the clenched fist ... you're full of hate, man!"

A trained skinhead in his forties sits down next to me and thinks he knows my whole story. He's scarred and I get chills from his penetrating gaze; the last time I saw eyes like this was in the faces of veterans from Sarajevo. I was there to protect a Serbian businessman who was living in Prague; they were paying their debts with diamonds; there were heaps of them. Each man had a bodyguard, a veteran of the Bosnian war, they all had something in common—something I had to pretend to share (and I know that I wasn't very convincing). They had the deep, unyielding look of those who had killed in cold blood.

"I'm looking for people who are able to fight. People who are scary like you – or me: yeah, I know myself as well as you know yourself. There's nothing wrong with that; quite the contrary. It's good to know that you have power, and that's where the fear comes from. The man I work for pays more than well ... what do you do for a living? if I may ask. Have you been in the army?"

"Sorry man, somehow I don't feel like talking to anyone today ... know what I mean? I'd rather be alone right now."

"Sure, I respect that. But I'll leave you my number anyway; one never knows, right? I won't bother you any more, I'll go sit over there."

Out of the blue, five gypsies walk into the smoky room looking from side to side and into the back. Heavyweights ... It seems like they're looking for skinheads. They look around the pub and their gaze fixes on me for a while at me, and then alights on the recruiter.

"Hey, we've got some Nazis here tonight. You're a Nazi, aren't you? And you too, back there."

The recruiter stands up, shoves the table forward a little to make more space, and stretches his neck.

"You hit the wrong joint tonight, skinhead."

The recruiter looks at me, and then looks back at them. I don't know what that was supposed to mean: does he expect me to help him? Why would I do that? This isn't my fight, and I'm not interested in Roma unless they come after me. All five are now standing in a semicircle around the recruiter. One of the Gypsies is still keeping an eye on me, to see if I'm going to get involved in the situation or not.

"Don't look at him, dickhead; he's not gonna help you!"

I can't see what's happening inside the semicircle properly, but I hear a familiar sound: a skull being smashed with a blunt object. It's clearer now: a telescopic nightstick has smashed through one gypsy's head. He falls between the tables. And now the storm lets loose. The remaining four gypsy heavyweights brutally beat the recruiter everywhere and every way they can. I can see a pint glass shattering over his head. But another pint glass smashes on the head of a big gypsy. In my hand, a wide shard remains. I hold it tight, and immediately slash another one in the throat; the blood gushes out of him, staining my face.

"Shit, you killed him, you bastard ... Laco, he killed my brother!"

I cut off his wail by taking another shard to his face. He sinks to his knees and tries to stop the blood spurting from his forehead with his hands. I don't feel like looking at him; I kick him in the head, just in case. In the meantime, the last attacker has disappeared. I didn't even notice him leave.

"Are you cool?" I give my hand to the recruiter and I raise him up to his feet. Staggering and bleeding he looks around the room.

"Jews or gypsies, it's the same scum ... they're everywhere. Absolutely ... everywhere."
I didn't take in the rest of the people in the pub. All the time, they sat silently at their tables, not moving a muscle. Now they're staring at us, their mouths wide open.

"Should I call an ambulance or something?" I say this more out of courtesy than concern, with an eye to the transfixed crowd.

"No need, gentlemen, they're on their way," interjects the proprietor, "and the cops too. We'll tell them everything that just happened." The recruiter then takes a swing at him and sends him back behind the counter. "Who the fuck asked you to do that? You fat idiot ... he called the cops, I've got to get out of here. Hey, don't forget the number I gave you," he reaches out his hand in a hurry. "My name's Heinrich. We'll definitely see each other again. And we'll pay for this, what you've proved here, in gold. You understand me?"

Heinrich? Interesting name – not common around these parts. I want to ask him again what kind of job it is exactly. I open the swing door to follow him into the hallway, but the recruiter with the German name has vanished. I can already hear the sirens of the ambulance, and the police too. No time now; I'd better get away from this place while I can.

CHAPTER 12: AFTER SOME TIME IN THE DARKNESS

"Hey, Paul, how come you don't have anyone?"

"Nobody said I didn't have anyone. Mom lives somewhere in Slovakia and my brother is in a medical institution there. He isn't well."

"And children? Where are they? How come you don't have any?"

"Maybe there are some, somewhere. Who knows? Up till now I've been living with whores. No ties of commitment."

"Yeah, I hear that. I like you, 'cause you know what? No one else is gonna miss you if something happens."

Heinrich is listening closely to my conversation with Kurt. He's leaning on the bar and refreshing himself with something that

I absolutely don't want any part of. In half an hour, we are setting off to another event. I need to be in peak condition for that.

"Listen up! You have a little less than three minutes. The task is to take down as many caps as..."

"What caps?" one skinhead speaks up from the crowd.

"The ones who have a kippah on their heads, chump. Should I also explain why they're wearing it? Fuck, what kind of a kindergarten class do I have today? I don't have the patience for this lot. Take over, Kurt."

Kurt continues:

"All right guys, listen up: we have three minutes. When you hear the whistle, scatter around the streets, so you don't run away in a group. Each of you knows his entrance: get there as quickly as possible, and then change your clothes. Then wait, and come out of the entrance and one by one. All of this will be filmed by our man sitting in one of the windows – so don't do anything stupid."

Heinrich is nervous today, more than I'd expect. I think it's because of the cameraman. He knows the neo-Nazi elite from all around the world are going to be watching. It seems to me that it's not such a big deal – just a vanity project – but he is wound up tight. He interrupts Kurt.

"This is going up on a big screen at the grand gathering. There'll be a huge celebration and medals will be awarded. And with medals comes money. So just don't screw up! Paul, you know what to do. You're here to provide us with extra assurance if we need it. So take care."

"Roger! Everything's clear!"

My job today is to ensure our protection. If the cops manage, by some chance, to catch a stray skinhead, I have to storm into the place and get him safely out of there. I feel myself breathing faster: adrenalin is already pumping through my body. No matches in a cage or ring come close to the thrill of taking part in a real event. Perhaps not even my experiences in the military can compare...

CHAPTER 13: MILITARY SCHOOL

Military school. Is this what they were preparing me for? An attack on a Jewish parade? I spent six years in isolation, training every day, for this? Military school...

"The whole Communist Party will be watching you, so heads up! This is an elite academy, boys; we'll be your only family for at least five years."

A little man in uniform is yelling at us out of the window. A group of thirty fourteen-year olds quietly follows an officer who's leading them out of the gate – where our mothers said goodbye to us for the last time – to the barracks.

"Halt! ... one – two!"

All of us bump into each other like dominos, but we don't go down. Someone laughs out loud, but most of us are silent. The terrified expression on many of our faces clearly shows that many of us didn't choose to come here voluntarily. We're facing a large building, built in the 1950s, waiting for them to let us in. In front of us, another thirty-member squad comes out, one boy after another, each with a large dark green bag in one hand and heavy high leather boots in the other; each one is shaved almost bald. And so we're standing in place and waiting. Each of us has his own story ... Mine seems to be running in an infinite playback loop in my head. It's too alive, too fresh to hit pause ...

CHAPTER 14: MEMORIES IN THE MEMORIES

"Mom, we're never gonna go back home to Slovakia, right?"

"You know how it is, Pauli."

"What did Dad mean when he said that we were in his apartment now, Mom?"

"He was right; we don't have anything at all."

"Couldn't we run away again? ... let's run away, Mom, I'll help with everything ... I promise ... and when we're in a village somewhere, I'll go and pick apples after school and help out in the collective farms to earn some money."

"You mustn't trust strangers Pauli, that's what the guy told you

that you'd be able to earn, the one who every now and then came to visit us when we were living with Mrs. Vera. He wasn't as nice as you think."
"And why did YOU trust Dad, Mom?"
Mum lowered her head ... pushing a stroller in front of her, up the hillside toward the cliff edge. I quicken my pace and catch up with her. She tries not to let me see, but I can see that she is crying.
"I'm very sorry ... forgive me ... I didn't know that he'd be like this."
... And we're up on the crest of the hill. Mom engages the brake on the stroller in which Jarry's sound asleep...
"Promise me that you'll stay together when they take you to the children's home ... you've got to take care of your brothers ... you promise?" "Don't cry, Mom ... who's gonna take us and where?"
"I know that he's beating you when I'm not at home ... she's panting ... why didn't you tell me? You don't trust me ... you're mad at me. I know that very well. Who stops him when I'm not there? One day he'll beat you to death."
"Maybe, Mom, it'd be better if they take just me and Miky away; he'll be nice to you and Jarry."
She begins to cry even harder; what have I done now? The truth is that Miky and I will be better off anywhere else than with our stepfather.
I know that when we get back from our walk, there'll be a big furor at home because of "something." I know that Miky is getting a beating right now, and that it started the moment we went out. Or maybe just now the beard-man is showering Miky with ice water so he doesn't fall asleep over his homework because he was studying until three in the morning last night. The insults, the sound of the hands falling hands on Miky's

body woke me up. Mom woke me up as she pleaded with Stepfather to let Miky go to sleep, saying that he'd definitely learn it tomorrow.

I know exactly what time it was. Mom's all dopey from those pills she takes; now she's a little dizzy and she's got a strange look on her face ... and her hair is a tousled nest.

/Slovak/ "Listen to me Pauli. Take the stroller with little Jarry and go home. I promise Dad's not gonna beat you ever again. Now, promise me that you'll take a look under the pillow when you get home, will you?" "What should I tell Dad when he asks where you are? He'll scream at me and blame me for again for leaving you alone."

/Slovak/ "You'll see that he won't this time ... just look under the pillow, will you? I'm just going to have a smoke... I'll be right back."

"I haven't heard you speak Slovak for so long, Mom. What's under the pillow? How do you know he'll never beat us again? Mum, are you listening to me?"

I think she has stopped paying attention to me; she's staring into the distance and drawing in the deepest puffs that I've ever seen her take. I wearily nod my head, then release the brakes of the stroller and slowly start to descend the slope.

"Forgive me, Pauli."

I hear those words from behind; of course that rotten old man's going to beat me; he'll be raving mad that Mom is hanging around outside ... and his dinner's not ready ... and God knows what else ...

/Slovak/ Forgive me, Pauli ... Screw this, Mom ... yeah, I'm pretty mad ... I don't like it here ... and a children's home? I've heard a lot about that... Miky and I can easily go there ... I answer angrily and loudly, in a language that I can only speak in my mind. Trying to articulate it, I stammer, but I manage to force out some words:

/Slovak/ "I can't, Mama ... I can't forgive."

I realize, half way down the hill that she told me to take care of the two younger boys. Did she mean Jarry as well? He doesn't have to go to children's home ... Stepfather wouldn't raise his hand against his own son ... he adores him. I've got to go look under the pillow as soon as I get home. The beard-man's not going to beat us again? I turn around to Mom – who in the meantime has disappeared.

"Mom..."

I run back up the hill, pushing the stroller with my little brother in front of me. My heart is pounding and my voice is shaking with despair as I shout. "Mom! ... Mom!"

I'm almost at the top ... a little bit further. I'm so relieved when I catch sight of her kneeling on the edge, looking back at me in confusion ... unsure if her son's voice is not just a hallucination.

/Slovak/ "Of course I'm not mad, Mom ... I didn't mean it like that ... really ... you can't leave us here all alone ... come home with me ... it'll all be different from now ... I promise ... you'll see ... come with us home, Mom."

That evening, when Miky was making the beds he found a suicidal farewell letter intended for us, the beard-man, and the Social Office. We meet our stepfather by chance on the way home. He is all hot and sweaty and ecstatically happy to see her. He hugs us, crying desperately.

"What's the matter with you? You know how worried I was about you? Come – there'll be a French comedy on TV tonight. A really funny one! And I've made potato pancakes."

He was very fond of her. He even loved us in his way. He wanted us not to embarrass him, and to grow up into polite and educated men – men he could be proud of. Over the years,

Miky and I had gotten used to the pain of punches and the sting of his belt on our skin ... what was cutting us up into pieces were his efforts to patch things up with us a few hours after a vicious beating. The apologies and explanations ... those efforts, for example, to stroke our hair at mealtimes, when we would instinctively react by covering our faces – a reflex that we couldn't get rid of for a number of years. To think that someone who could sometimes be so kind and even thoughtful could also be so mean and brutal to frightened children. Distrust of everything good was the result of those childhood years. As a child I read somewhere: "People can be nice and kind, magnanimous and generous when they are in front of the smallest audience, and cruel and heartless, cynical and unscrupulous when no one is looking." I was a witness to this phenomenon my whole childhood. Yet I knew that there were some people who weren't covered by this dictum. I called these rare specimens..."angels."

The idyll lasted less than a week. We travelled together by train on the trip, and Dad took us out for ice cream. Then everything started over again, the only difference being that Miky and I turned the screaming at night down to a minimum, each time assuring Mom that the bruises, which she couldn't help but notice, came from fights at school or falls during physical education. Mom was happy. She believed that in the end we had come to an understanding with the beard-man ... and we didn't say anything to her and never complained, for fear of what she might do. But if steam keeps building up in a pot and clogs the valve, it eventually explodes.

CHAPTER 15: AFTER A FEW YEARS...

Stepfather is on a rampage today, screaming at everyone. "I told you – in no uncertain terms – that you had to pass those tests ... or do you think I'm kidding? Once more: get back to your room. You've got another half hour to learn how the equation is calculated. You hear me, stupid? If you don't show it to me when you come out, you'll end up riding with the garbage men; but even worse, you'll disgrace me in the neighborhood!"

A few days later, Miky passes the exams for the bricklayers' vocational school, though he'd rather go to the railway high school – locomotives always attracted him. He could spend hours sitting with our Bratislava granny at the station observing the trains, and waiting for the dispatcher to give the "go" signal to the driver. He always wanted to be an engine driver; but who cares about fulfilling the wishes of a child? We'd seen his wish fulfilled once, only to be cruelly taken away. A parent's job is to know what's best for their kids, despite what they may wish for. "Milovan, your half hour's up, so come over here! Or do I have to go get you?"

Miky, frightened, comes into the living room; mathematics never went well for him, though I think it was stress that usually prevented him from understanding the equations rather than innate inability to learn this subject. Like many other children, he was afraid to ask for an explanation for lack of having ever known someone with the patience to break the problems down slowly into their component parts. There are so few good teachers, and his had been worse than average. Stepfather dictates an exercise. Miky sits at a table and writes. "Come on, now ... your five minutes are running out. Don't screw it up again!"

I'm polishing shoes in the hall – every Saturday they all have to be as spotless as alabaster, as the beard-man puts it. I prick up my ears when Miky starts on the timed exercises in the living room. He lowers his head and begins to cry: he can't work under this kind of pressure. I can feel it, the tension before the explosion ... I'm looking at them from the hall, and I know that this moment is another crossroads. Taking this turn means the road to the station marked "easy happiness" closes.

A hand, bigger than a paddle, slams into Miky's head. His glasses, flying through the air, crash onto the television. Miky starts wailing and pleading:
"Dad, please ... nooo ..."

One blow after another hits the bony little body that is trying to hide under the table. The enraged beard-man tosses the table aside and shouts: "I'm gonna beat it into you, you stupid bastard!"

This is unendurable. Am I strong enough to walk through the valley of the shadows? Am I strong enough to withstand a heavyweight fight? I don't know. The determination and rage flowing in my blood smash these questions like the brick that a few days earlier – after years of hard training – I broke for the first time.

I throw away the beard-man's huge, reeking, unpolished shoe and plunge myself into a battle with the 280-lb savage who robbed us of our carefree childhood. I get up from the ground as fast as I can and charge into him with all my strength. He staggers. He loses his balance and slams his shoulder into the glass showcase on top of the cabinet. The glass shatters and the shards fall on the carpet. The beard-man is bleeding heavily. I stand over him frightened by the blood and havoc that I have caused. Miky crawls to the opposite corner of the room. For a moment we just stare at each other. Then suddenly a giant force raises me into the air and slams me into the wall. The sound I make crying out is cut off, because I cannot breathe anymore. I am still winded when Stepfather picks me up and throws my hundred-pound frame across the living room toward where Miky is hiding. I hit the ground right next to him, wheezing, desperately trying with all my strength to breathe. The colossus turns around quickly and starts thrashing me like an angry gorilla. I protect my face and allow my reflexes to move my blocks where needed. Just a while longer and I'll be able to breathe again.

I remember one training session with my first teacher, a renowned local brawler, who beat me in the stomach with a log in the woods, while I stood with my fists pressed into my armpits. The stick creates an unpleasant barbed pain and a few times, when I exhaled badly, it smashed the oxygen out of my lungs.

"What is it? Solar plexus? You have to bend backwards and then quickly back. You don't know pain! You hear? The ninja doesn't feel pain!"

Those movies like ninja games are probably saving my life now. The beard-man catches me by the leg and pulls me onto the balcony. He wants to throw me off the third floor, the coward! I grab onto the doorframe, kicking as hard as I can; suddenly I'm free again. I'm on my feet. I start to run away from him, but immediately I stop myself: I won't run away any more!

I turn and stand in a combat position, with one hand covering my chin and the other, clenched into a fist, pointing at my hated enemy.

"You're gonna try some of your positions on me, you bastard?" He throws himself at me. I'm on my guard, waiting for him, then deliver a side kick called Yoko Geri. I dig the heel of my foot into beard-man's navel, which in his case would be better termed a paunch. I'd thrown this kick into a tree in the woods maybe a thousand times, but his belly offers much less resistance, and he's off balance. The beard-man flies back through the doors to the balcony, which he had closed behind him. At that moment Mom rushes into the room; she has returned from shopping with Jarry. Registering the bloodstains on the walls and the smashed furniture, now in pieces on the carpet, she shrieks in terror. Miky's huddled in the corner crying and Jarry, the gorilla's spoiled son, throws himself at me hatefully. I'm in a trance ... my body is controlled by my subconscious, so with the same side kick I send the eight-year old to his knees. He hits the ground and doesn't move. Mom, screaming, tries to resuscitate him, and thank God she does it. The balcony door swings open one last time, this time so hard that it hits the wall and the rest of the shards, which had only been hanging by threads along the sides, fly into the air and hit Mom in the face.

Now everyone's yelling. I'm standing in my position, waiting to see what's going to come rushing in from the balcony. Stepfather, covered in blood, hurls himself at me with a speed no one would expect from a man of his size. I can't use the kick, my best weapon, with him so close ... He grabs me by the throat with both hands, picks me up and crushes me against the wall with his full weight and starts strangling me with all his strength. Time slows down again ...

I remember scenes from childhood ... Racing with Miky on the lawn behind our apartment building in Bratislava, laughing. I see Peter and my beloved Drahuška encouraging us; I can see my dear Papa, as he returns from work with his briefcase. We all have a smile on our faces, we're all so happy there ... I'm slowly returning to the world of memories. My eyes close and I begin to see a beautiful white light.

I don't know exactly what pulls me back. I suddenly look at my stepfather ... I look into his angry, reddened, bulging eyes – he looks like he's out of his mind.

Enough!

My palms clench into fists, the joints of my forefingers shoot up out of my fists and my thumbs secure them: The Japanese call these fists "Iponken". I start beating the bloodthirsty savage beast wherever I can. His grip loosens and the joints of my index fingers begin to impact on his terrified eyes at the speed of sound. One blow after another falls, as if I'm holding a machine gun trigger, using up the entire magazine in a few seconds.

He lets go of me; finally, I can feel the floor again. My Adam's apple is crushed into my neck, but the pain no longer concerns me now. The ferocious beast falls onto the carpet among the shards. I throw myself on him, my fists continuing to fall on his Goliath body. There is whistling in my ears; the sound drowns out the screams of everyone in the room. I can feel the policemen and neighbors from the floor below tearing me away and pulling me into the hall, where everyone is now kneeling around me. I scream that I'll kill him, I'll cut his throat. Everything's blurry, colors and sounds; I can see men in white coats run through the hallway to the living room, more and more figures come ...

And then there's silence, after the short stabbing of a needle I don't even feel...

"Third Platoon, on my command ... attention! I will call your name and you will reply: 'here!' Then in formation and on the instruction of the platoon leader you will move to your quarters, where you will be shown only once how to put things in your wardrobe. Whoever has spent the last hour gazing into space, you have done so for the first and the last time. I am a corporal; when I address you, you will answer me, 'yes, Comrade Corporal!' Do you understand?"

"Yes, Comrade Corporal!"

"Bacil..."

"Here!"

"Batel ..."

"Here!"

"Blažek ..."

"Here!"

I admit that, at the beginning, military life felt restrictive, but I soon began to prefer the loud commands, the discipline, and the constant training to living at home. At least the rules and the consequence for breaking them were clear and understood by all here. And I remember how, after a few months of training, our rookie squad was dropped into a deep forest with a kit of full-combat gear: a bag full of things that should ensure survival anywhere. The helicopter hovered fifteen meters above the ground; one cadet would descend a rope; then the helicopter would fly on for another minute and repeat the process. Thirty fourteen-year old cadets soon found themselves a hundred meters from each other in every direction. The goal was to find each other and form a unit, then together to trace a path back toward civilization and telephone to report the location for a pickup. The mission took us two nights and three days. And the whole platoon, one hundred and fifty scouts, was continually monitoring us, without our ever realizing it. A platoon of fifth-year elite soldiers, in perfect camouflage, was watching each of us every minute. Their mission was to keep tabs on two freshman squads in complete secrecy. It was all so real and exciting; in tandem with the continuous training, there were exams every day. Everybody studied, and when the going got hard with schoolwork everybody helped each other to understand the math, chemistry, and physics they were teaching us. The area where we lived, isolated from civilians, was huge and perfectly equipped for training. In the evenings outside, groups of friends and rivals could be seen training. Some did pull-ups, others exercised on the parallel bars, and other boys would run around the track. This was a perfect place to live an orderly, structured life without any real-world troubles.

Around the site there was a long high wall and beyond it, on the civilian side, patrols of soldiers doing their compulsory military service as guards. They were vigilant: they knew that if they managed to catch one of us they'd be allowed to go home on leave as a reward. Believe me, that was a great motivator in those days! Compulsory service lasted for two years, and soldiers were always stationed at the opposite end of the country from their homes. Back then the country was still, of course, Czechoslo- vakia. Did you come from the "left" end of the state? Then they sent you to the "right," twelve hundred kilometers from home. You could see your parents or a girlfriend every three months if you were an exceptional soldier; for example, if you caught a future elite communist officer "aban- doning his crew." Otherwise you could enjoy the comforts of home once every six months.

They didn't like us at all, those involuntarily conscripted soldiers. They knew the school was training officers who'd be tough and uncompromising with people like them. They also had to make do with smaller quarters than us. The height of the wall that divided our worlds was reduced in only one place: the kitchen. We would pass by them at lunchtime. They would just march away, retreating from the wall, putting distance be- tween themselves and us. Once every so often, instructions would be circulated through the hall during breakfast for everyone to save their container of yogurt or milk from lunch. Everyone knew what that meant: preparation for war. It would be announced by an attack on the wall in front of the entrance to the dining room. Although there were eight hundred of us at school, lunch was divided into two batches of four hundred: the first-year students would march with the second-years, the third-years with the fourth-years. The company commanders would give a command at the wall: "Halt!" And out of the crowd the order would come:

"Officers of the academy, prepare to attack!"

Four hundred guys would put their hands into their uniforms and pull out milk grenades. On average, this would happen twice a year. It was a nightmare for our commanders. Confused they would run between us shouting at us to stop. From the crowd you would then hear one of the living legends among the older grades (mostly multiple winners of our own no-rules fight club) calling out:

"target the enemy with a single volley over the wall; fire at my com- mand!"

Four hundred cups of yogurts or plastic containers of milk would fly at the enemy. The fighting started every time one of those bastards caught an upperclassman as he was climbing over the wall, usually to visit his girlfriend who was waiting for him in a nearby park. When one of us was caught, it meant two to three days in jail, sometimes without light; but no one was taken seriously until he went through solitary confinement. The worst part was after the release. It was necessary to immediately catch up with the schoolwork, because the next day you were tested mercilessly; you only had one night to learn everything. Bad grades? That means mandatory tutoring in the evenings, which would prevent you from enjoying the only free time ever provided.

And so the war began every time our neighbors caught a fugitive – and gave him a humiliating beating in front of his girlfriend. Often those twenty-year old lechers would also touch and strip the cadet's fifteen-year old girlfriend while he had to watch. So wars would be declared, fights would break out, and ugly confrontations would take place at night. They would try to defend themselves, to invade our territory in retaliation. Of course, their efforts were in vain. Our training was elite and our patrols astute and always alert. Participants in these fights were hailed as heroes – everyone knew their names.

In the third year I proudly ranked among them, along with my best friend, Petr Novak. At military school I learned what true friendship looks like.

I remember when I won the military league championship in combat; I thought back to a scene in court.

"Look, Paul ... you really hurt your stepfather. According to the testimonies of neighbors, teachers, and classmates it is known that you have been training regularly in preparation for injuring or seriously hurting him. I am therefore categorizing you as problematic and dangerous to society; no doubt you deserve to be sent to a detention center for sociopathic youth. However, I am also taking into account your excellent performance at school, which you owe to the injured party, your stepfather, and I am sending you to Czechoslovakia's elite military school."

Where was the audience who used to listen to the rows in our apartment from the street? Those who knew about the daily and nightly drubbings Miky and I were subjected to and might have spoken a word in my defense.

Nowhere.

CHAPTER 16: FROM MEMORIES BACK INTO REALITY

The Jewish procession – a tribute to the victims of the Holocaust – is approaching. In the middle march rabbis, singing. As they draw near, the singing becomes louder and louder. Suddenly the call comes:

"AT THEM!"

So it begins. Twenty trained neo-Nazi soldiers in green jackets and heavy boots pounce on the shocked crowd of mostly young Jews, both men and women. They fall down like chess pieces as the knuckledusters break their jaws. There is chaos everywhere and the girls are screaming hysterically, running in every direction. It reminds me of a chicken coop being attacked by wolves. Heinrich's assistant Kurt films everything carefully on his own video camera – just in case the professional in the window fails. With a devious smile he keeps his concentration fixed on the events so as not to miss any of the "best" moments. I'm standing on the hood of the car, where I jumped as soon the attack began. Looking over the entire scene, I can see some of the Jews attempting to defend themselves. I watch young men trying to shield their girlfriends with their bodies. The skinheads lay into them as hard as they can. After a moment they cease; a mess of men and hats lies in a pool of blood on the ground. One 140-kilo neo-Nazi spreads his arms and takes off into the crowd of girls, mow- ing them down with his weight. One of the Jewish women has long hair, which gets tangled in his knuckleduster; he drags her along the ground a few meters. The girl is screaming, begging him to let her go.

Then, finally, the Jewish security men enter the fray and converge on the giant. They beat him with steel batons. As the giant falls to the ground, his pleading, desperate eyes look into mine. It seems that my time has come. I jump down from the hood of the car and accelerate towards the Jewish resistance. Leaping into the air I take out one of them with a flying kick. He flies several meters, bounces on the ground, and takes several old rabbis down with him. I hit the second one with a cut into his Adam's apple. The other two, who are still beating the giant neo-Nazi, throw themselves at me. I wait until they're close enough and then kick that little squirt – the fool who thought that he could threaten a fighter who has trained with elite soldiers every day for his whole life – in his crotch. With a cry, he recoils and falls to the ground screaming. Meanwhile, the other manages to swing at me with an open hook, but misses; before he can take another hit, a passing neo-Nazi with a chain wrapped round his fist catches him with a punch to his jaw. A loud whistle ends this bloodbath, which leaves countless helpless, dazed, and crawling bodies on the ground.

All the fascists scatter exactly as planned, then regather a few streets away, behind doors and gates left unlocked for them by accomplices in the Old Town. Their loyal messengers are waiting there with fresh clothes. Having changed, they quietly slip into the parked cars and taxis that are unobtrusively waiting for them. I leave in a taxi with Heinrich. Only now can the sirens of the police cars be heard. But the attackers have all gone, as though they had disappeared into thin air.

Perfect event, perfect plan, perfect execution. And how do I feel? I'm leaving in a taxi with Heinrich and I have a feeling that I had spotted in Judge Kaufman in the crowd, falling to the ground in panic with her husband. That same bitch Kaufman who, without hesitation, took away my right to see my little princess. My only light in the darkness of an other-wise meaningless life.

Did you know that when you take an angel's light away he becomes a demon?

I'm going to continue to protect the servants of what was once such a powerful and dark nothingness. Today I wasn't much needed. But soon my time is going to come – I can feel it.

"Hiya, Daddy!"

"Hey baby, come to me!" She flies into my arms, that little princess of mine; I hold her tight, I can smell the scent of her hair. Our three-hour session starts. We'll enjoy it to the fullest.

"Mr. Batel, I wanted to tell you that today Maria was terribly naughty when we went for a swim. She screamed and fought – nothing would convince her to get in the water."

"Excuse me? I can't explain that, she likes to swim after all. Did she get into the water in the end?"

"Well, we finally pulled her in by force in front of the whole kindergarten, so she had to go. Her mother paid for her lessons and we don't want any complaints."

Maria is standing next to me, hiding her head so that the teacher can't see her. I think that the problem is that Maru doesn't like this lady.

"Let me tell you something: when Maria doesn't want to go swimming, don't force her. She must have a reason for it. I pay for these lessons, so don't worry about what her mother says. Do you understand me? Next time just leave her with those who don't go swimming."

"I ... I thought ... well ... sometimes you have to give the kids tough love so they don't get spoiled."

"You give that "tough" treatment to human waste. Is that what you think that Maru is?"

"I'm sorry, I ... I didn't mean any harm. I – "

"Do you know the feeling you get when you break a little girl's spirit and she agrees to along with the others out of fear of you? With Maria, you have felt that for the last time!"

I don't even know what came over me ... how I behave ... a lot of things have changed since I've stopped working. A sense of injustice and a strange desire for violence have gradually begun to devour me, until very little is left. I'm quiet most of the day; I don't speak at all when I don't have to. I cannot remember the last time I laughed. These three hours with my little girl are the only light that prevents me from getting lost in the darkness – it gives me hope that all of this is only temporary. I now live under the highway in a former railway house that dates from 1901. The guy who owns the parking lot has rented me two rooms, one above the other. I have a gym downstairs, where I train to keep in shape, and I sleep in the attic. The sink and shower, which provide no hot water, are downstairs;

there's no toilet. When necessary, I stretch a plastic bag over the trash can, and then throw it into a dumpster outside the parking lot; nothing complicated. The need for the comfort of rented apartments disappeared with my bodyguard job. A year and a half to go until the court order restricting me to seeing Maru once a month expires, along with the suspension of my weapons license. Then I'll have a real job again and everything will be like it was before.

We go to the park. There are plenty of monkey bars and a pyramid net, which is good for strengthening the entire body: she likes that one. She can climb up to the top all by herself. I watch from inside the ropes, just in case something goes wrong. Then we build a sand castle and dig a tunnel. Maru comes up with the idea to fill it with water. We talk and time passes quickly.

"Dad? The teacher won't be hard on me, right? She was afraid of you; even Stepfather Alois is afraid of you, and Mom too. I heard them talking yesterday evening in the living room. Someday I'll be as strong as you. People will be afraid of me and will do what I tell them."

"Bubu, it doesn't work that way; people are afraid of me because they're stupid. They're afraid of what they see on the surface, they're scared of what they imagine to be strength. Believe me, it's not like that."

"What is it then to be strong?"

"I'll explain it to you some time; you're too small for that now. But you'll be different from me, you'll see. People will love you, respect you, you know. They'll do what you say because you ask them nicely; you won't have to repeat it, they'll gladly do it for you. Next time the teacher is strict with you, ask her nicely to stay with the others. Don't fight her – you'll see that it'll work."

"But she's so mean!"

"Remember that only the strongest can stand against evil. You're not there yet, so you have to be smart. Use your little head – be nice and kind, let the teacher think she has won. Think about this, Bubu, promise?" "No!"

"You little warrior! Come to me, so I can hold you for a while. I have to take you home soon."

"Dad? Will I see you tomorrow?"

"No, not tomorrow, nor the day after tomorrow."

"The day after that?"

"Not the day after, Bubu ... we'll see each other in a month. But don't worry, the time will pass quickly."

What am I supposed to say to her? Should I lie to her? Or say that sometimes when one day drags after another, a month can take forever? Especially when one counts every day and waits. Should I tell her that her mother's a bitch who's planning a new family with a stranger, and that she believes this little one must adopt a new father and slowly forget about the old one? She begins to cry softly.

My heart wrenches inside, and I'm going back to my childhood, as if time has stopped. I can see myself back with Miky again, as we run around the house in Bratislava with Peter and Drahuška. I'm almost eight years old. In the evening in the children's room Mom gives out clean pajamas; as we're changing, she notices that I have a rash on my hand. Those nasty blisters are growing and spreading, and they're itching like mad.

CHAPTER 17: THAT "NICE" DAD AT THE END OF OUR TIME IN BRATISLAVA

"Well, young man, I think you'd better go to the hospital."
To the hospital? What can the doctor mean? Because there are pimples on my hand that are turning into blisters? It looks gruesome and it itches, but hopefully an ointment of some sort will take care of it, won't it?
"We have to look at it close up to see whether it is really just a reaction to a Band-Aid or something else; there is nothing we can do otherwise." Mom peeks at me with a sad look, helps me back into my shirt, and takes the slip that she is to hand in at the hospital. I've never been in hospital before. Tomorrow's

Friday and Papa's supposed to pick us up! How long will I have to stay there? I'm a little scared.

It's morning and my Dad says he'll go with me and tells me I'll carry my suitcase myself since I'm already such a big guy. And no tears: men don't cry, of course.

"Well don't you worry; your Papa's not gonna run away. He cancelled the visit anyway because he had a lot of work to do. In the meantime, Milovan's going to be studying with Mom at home."

I have no idea that Mom has called Papa to tell him that we are sick and that he can't come for another three weeks. But something isn't right; it doesn't ring true to me. I don't believe a word that the beard-man said: Papa wouldn't just blow us off because of work. I'm sitting on the trolleybus with the beard-man, feeling anxious. I feel like crying because I'm afraid of the unknown, but I can't give in – it always makes Milord of Prague see red. I'm sitting on the seat and clinging to my briefcase. I couldn't take any toys with me because supposedly it's forbidden. Moreover, I'll be eight soon, and big guys don't need any toys.

When we arrive at the hospital, a lady in a white coat takes the note the doctor gave Mom. Stepfather takes me inside; he's being kind and supportive.

"Don't you get worried, man, I'll come and visit you, even if your own daddy has walked out on you. See, you have someone who really loves you. I'll come back in a few days."

I put down the suitcase and throw myself into his arms. My tears are falling down and I'm so sorry that I'm treating him unjustly, and that my own Papa's not with me. In the end that man from Prague might not be so bad. I actually kind of like him – he has never hit me: he just shouts and complains to Mom sometimes. Sometimes we don't want to obey him right away, but the routine that he set up at home actually makes sense to me. He always says he means well, he doesn't want us to grow up to be crooks or losers. And we've got to be smart, so I have actually come to prefer studying to running around outside with my friends. He's ... the only one I've got here now. The lady in a blue and white coat prompts me: "So let's go, we've got to change and the consultant expects to see you in one hour."

The lady in a blue and white coat leads me down a long dark corridor. We enter a large room, which contains what seems like an infinite number of cribs with bars around them. I am too anxious to answer when the nurse asks me, "Your dad is from Czech Republic, right? What a nice dad you have." "That's not my dad, he's a dad from Prague. My Papa couldn't come today, because he's got a lot of work."

Nobody is around; the whole vast, dark room is just for me alone. After a few days I find a corner by the window overlooking the garden. From now on, it's my place, where I remember what it was like when we still lived with Papa all together. It's just fragments, but I carefully protect them so I don't forget. I miss him so much; he never shouts, he's always kind, and he listens attentively to the stories I tell him from our school. When he takes us back on Sunday after a weekend every two weeks, I run to the window in the kitchen, waving at him until he passes out of sight. He turns around every five meters and waves back at me. I often ask Mom why they're not together anymore, and if it could somehow be worked out for them to be together again. Mom always says she doesn't want to talk about it and sends me away to go play.

Sometimes I feel very sorry about it, especially when the new Dad shouts and is strict. Some things that bother him are when we clean up the room the wrong way, and when he finds that the dishes aren't completely dry after we washed them. He screams that I am undeserving and have no respect for anything when I unintentionally break an old toy that after so many years happens to fall apart in my hands. So I sit by the window on a bench, thinking and remembering. And the days out there fly by.

"A visitor, Pauli! Your dad's come!" Papa? He found out that I was in the hospital and finally came to see me! I dash into the hallway and run to the front door. It's not Papa, though – stupid nurse! It's Dad.

"Hey man, how's it going? Look what I've brought you, seeing as your old man doesn't give a damn about you. Chocolate! Aren't you glad? I know you're sorry he hasn't come, but you've got me, right?"

I nod and silently take the chocolate. Tears have returned to my eyes, even though I know I mustn't cry.

"Well, well, what is it?"

"Yes, I know, guys don't cry."

"Well, there you go. You had better hurry back so the nurse won't be mad at you. You have pretty nurses here, huh?"

Quietly I answer "yes" because no one else is with me in that huge room. I won't talk about that with you, I think, and slowly crawl back down the corridor, heading to my window. This chocolate is going to be good, I'd better save it – that's what the Prague dad teaches us. Chocolates are just for birthdays, Christmas, or as a major, major reward. So I'm sitting at the window, watching the children from other blocks play in the sandbox and on the monkey bars; watching birds chase each other among the branches of monumental trees and dash into the bushes. Between them, there's a gap of about two meters and that creates another window, through which I can see as far as the roofs of the old town of Bratislava. Sometimes, I can't see anything through the trees; other times, when the weather's nice, I can even see the inverted pyramid building where my Papa works. Somewhere there in the office he's preparing the evening news for the radio and the television. If only he'd come to visit; he wouldn't even have to bring chocolate, I just want him to come. Surely he didn't blow me off, he just has a lot of work, writing the news. This new gentleman, who loves it when I call him "Dad" in Czech isn't always so bad, and he can be nice in a strange way. Like the teacher in kindergarten, who suddenly became nice when she declared that the children whose parents didn't come were going to have a two-hour nap. Nobody liked sleeping in kindergarten, but no one objected – because the teacher was being so gentle.

During those three weeks, Dad comes two more times, each time for five minutes. He talks about how my Papa blows me off and is not interested in me at all. I think I'm getting better; I want to cry again when Dad says all those things about Papa, but I resist – until I can't stop the tears.

"I know, Pauli, it's hard for you, to know that your father doesn't visit his own son when he's miserable in the hospital ... I know. You know, you've got to learn to appreciate people – the people who don't forget you. Anyway, I've got to take off. I was talking to the doctor and he said that any day now they'll let you go home. A big surprise is being prepared for you, it's gonna be quite something."

What is it he said? To appreciate people? What did he mean by that? That my Papa's actually someone who's indifferent to me? That he really doesn't care about me? That's why he hasn't come and isn't coming? Why is he saying all that? How can he be so sure!?

Day after day goes by, evening after evening. When am I going home?

"You are healthy, Paul; our fears were thankfully unfounded – you just had an allergic reaction to a Band-Aid. We were afraid that you had a rare infection; that's why we kept you in quarantine. You have handled this very bravely; all of the nurses were amazed. Tomorrow morning you will go home; you must be looking forward to it!"

Finally, I'm spending my last night in the hospital. For the last time I'm looking at the garden from my window and thinking about what I'll say to Papa when I see him. The day after tomorrow will be Friday and he'll definitely come and pick me up. I won't know what face to wear; he'll probably be able to tell that I'm angry at him. Will he pretend nothing has happened? Will he be glad to see me and ask, as always, where we should go on Saturday? I love our trips! Despite everything, I'm still looking forward to seeing him so much ...

"Listen to me, Bubu: never believe anyone who tells you that I don't love you and that I don't want to see you. It's not true, and it never will be! Don't argue with them if they tell you that, just nod your head; let them think that you believe them. Only you and I will know that the truth is the opposite – deal?" Maru is still crying quietly.

"They're already saying it. Mom says it, even Granddaddy and Aunt Roza." I suspected this. It's amazing how the past repeats itself. I won't let it be like this; I'll save up for the best damned lawyer money can buy – the best! I'll be able to take my little Maria out three times a week again. I'll take that job offered by Heinrich, or whatever he's called ... I'll take it.

I don't like Jews after all; they let my father die, and now they've taken my little girl. This way I'll be among my own people and also make a lot of money. It seems like a good plan.

"Don't cry ... Daddy's gonna come up with something. Soon it'll be just like before, don't you worry about a thing. Remember, Maru: just nod your head when they say nasty things about Daddy! You have to be smarter than they are. I know you can handle it."

CHAPTER 18: SOON THE PAST BECOMES MY FUTURE

The telephone wakes me up. What time is it? Nine? I'm all sore after yesterday's pummeling; I bruised my shin and my thumb on some Jew. I was probably holding my fist down wrong. Damn ... who's calling at this hour in the morning? DJ from the agency?

"Hey, man, you haven't called in a long time. Don't tell me you have a contract for me, without a gun license."

"You better believe it, Paul. Well actually no one will know that you don't have a handgun. We won't go telling them. This is a cool gig: big wheels from America, Jews. You've got them for two days – Tuesday in Prague, visiting some sights, a lunch, a meeting at the Jewish center-there they'll be singing or whatever – then a dinner and another meeting with the top Jews in Prague. After that, there'll be an interview of some sort, then back to the hotel and away."

"DJ, my man, you've got no idea how grateful I am that you're calling me, even though you know how things are. I really appreciate it. I just don' know if it's a good idea to show up in a Jewish center ... "

"Wait, Paul, you mean you don't want it? Hell, I thought that you'd leap at this: you're out of your job, bro, the money's great, and the job's a piece of cake. Or have you got something against the Jews? Have you heard the news? You know what happened yesterday in the Jewish Quarter."

"No ... I don't listen to the news and I don't have an aerial, so I don't even watch TV. What happened last night?"

"Man, Paul, you live like an animal in a cave. You better find some kind of temporary job till they give you back your gun license. Listen: yesterday the Jews had a procession and were attacked by neo-Nazis ... about ten people ended up in the hospital on IV drips. The perps then vanished into thin air before the cops came ... they were well organized. So you get why the Jews want some protection."

"Sure, DJ, of course I'll take it. I'm awfully glad you're calling me, really glad. Send me the details in a message, OK?"

"Finally you're coming to your senses, Paul. The next day you're going to Terezín, so the hours won't be so long. You'll have a break there for about two hours while the Jews are tucked away in some barracks; they'll have local guards there. Hey, let's grab a beer together soon, yeah? Meantime, I'll call them about the dough. Ciao ... and take care of yourself."

I knew it had been a good idea to put a scarf over my face ... what if somebody in the Jewish center recognizes me?

But of course that's silly. I'll be wearing a suit, not a bomber jacket. What was he saying? Ten people on drips? Just as well they didn't finish anyone off. Are you ready for this? You think they're gonna let you go when the contract runs out, just let you go back to your real job? And what about Maru? How are you going to see her when you're somewhere in Germany with Heinrich? More to the point: do you really want to leave?

CHAPTER 19: CONTRACT

"Isn't it strange, but you know you look so familiar to me. As if I knew you from somewhere; it's amazing how some people can resemble each other. I could swear I know you from somewhere, or maybe you have a double. But sorry; I'm just an old man. What can we do about it when the moment comes after such a long time waiting? But don't worry, I'm sure you learned to use your combat knife in the military."

"Oh boy, professor, you're speaking in verse. Or does it only seem like it? What do you mean?"

"I'm sorry, sometimes it just starts by itself. It has been a long time since I wrote poems, a very long time. Anyway, you have been in the army, haven't you? Judging by the short haircut and the way you look. However, young man, there is no war here. And yet it seems to be that you want to be in battle? So why have you left the army?"

"I don't know. Maybe I didn't fancy obeying the endless orders any more. Perhaps with communism gone, the threat was gone too. They began reducing the number of soldiers. They stopped sending us on exercises and we began to rot in the barracks. Outside, people were laughing at us, saying that we were slackers and freeloaders. The prestige of being an elite soldier has evaporated. I had no idea that a few years after I left they would start the missions to Iraq and Afghanistan and troops would be needed again. I don't regret my decision, professor; I've became a personal bodyguard and a combat teacher."

"That is interesting; so whom do you guard most often, if I may ask?" "Well ... sort of anyone who needs an eye kept on them ... traders who are afraid because they've got into trouble... actresses who are threatened by perverts or former partners ... politicians who don't trust government-issued protection – all kinds of clients."

"So: the good and the bad. Well that is interesting indeed. Are not you afraid that you will become bad too when you protect such people?" "Excuse me, professor. I'm going to see if the film has ended yet."

"You don't have to, I've ordered two films for our clients – a propaganda movie that the Nazis shot here, and a documentary about the history. We have another forty minutes."

"Still I'd rather look into it ... excuse me."

All the time he's looking at me so weirdly. I'm afraid that he may have recognized me from the attack on the Jewish procession; he might have been there too. Next time I'll have to camouflage myself better. It doesn't seem right; I've got to admit that I'll be glad when this contract ends. There are too many Jews around me; that's not a good feeling. The clients are sitting in the cinema hall; the Terezín Museum is half empty. Not many people come here, apparently. Who's interested in this story? Perhaps we should move forward and not keep looking back to what happened sixty years ago. DJ was right, this contract looks like a piece of cake. I'll pop back down to the snack bar after all and have one more coffee with the professor.

"So what about our guys, nobody has kidnapped them?"

"Not yet. You got to be tired after all that guiding and talking to our special V.I.P clients. Care for some more coffee, professor?"

"No, thank you, Paul. At my age it is not good to drink so much coffee. Here where we are sitting, children are peeling potatoes; boys, mostly naughty boys who had done something. It has been so long and, you see? I'm still here."

Nostalgically he glances around over the snack bar; then his gaze turns back to me. This does nothing to calm me down, that resigned smile of his.

"Did you know there are hidden corridors here? Sometimes even three underground floors: down below us is a whole labyrinth: one can easily get lost there," he says with a twinkle in his eye.

"Hallways? How would they get here?"

"Two hundred years ago, Terezín was the best fortress in the world, Mr. Paul. Habsburg soldiers could relocate underground whenever necessary. In case of a siege they could live underground for months. The tunnels actually lead several kilometers away from here. They could circumvent the enemy any time, or disappear from the fortress entirely."

"That's fascinating, professor. I'm quite interested in these things." "Would you like to see a tunnel?"

"What? You mean..."

"Well, yes, of course, it's impossible for the public to look inside. They're all barred and locked – they're dangerous, you know."

"Now I don't quite follow you, professor. How can you show me such a tunnel then?"

Old fool, now he is gazing into space, his mind is somewhere else. Well he sure has a sense of drama. His face suddenly becomes earnest and his expression petrified.

"I've got a key, Mr. Paul... I've got a key."

"Professooor? Halloooo. I can't see anything. Why have you turned off the flashlight? Where are you? Ouch. God damn it." I've bumped into something. We've been descending for quite some time. We've gone round a lot of corners. The professor seems to have disappeared into thin air. I find myself in a hallway, where the air is getting colder.

As I move forward, I feel like I'm descending even further into the earth. I try to come back slowly, but soon I'm heading back downhill again. Shit – must have taken a turn somewhere. I can't see anything at all, not even a ray of light. How the soldiers could operate down here I have no idea. Perhaps there's a light switch or something. If only I hadn't left my cell phone in the car. There's nothing to light my way, and that's not good at all. How could we lose each other so suddenly? Heck, I've stepped in something. It smells of diesel. I'm starting to get a little nervous. I have to keep to the wall and follow it slowly.

"Professooor??!!" I'm calling him, and hurling curses at him, at the top of my voice. He said that there are over twenty kilometers of underground corridors here. Surely I haven't covered more than three hundred meters? I must still be near the entrance. Perhaps I should just stand in one place and wait. Don't panic. Just relax. Think. Do I have a lighter? That smell was diesel or gasoline or something: combustible fumes. I don't have a light anyway. Damn.

Now I must've been here for several hours. Waiting is useless. I'll try to keep going slowly step by step, I'll stick to the wall. What's that? There's actually a hole. I can't put my weight on the ground. All right, move back slowly, just don't panic. I'm still sweating, but it's from the stress. That old codger must've called for help by now. What's this again? Now I'm stepping on something wooden. The wall vanishes, I can't find it by touch anymore – the tunnel is becoming broader. Is that some sort of a bridge? Where the hell am I supposed to go?

"Heeelp! Halloooo....! Heeelp!"
Stop it, immediately! Just stop being hysterical. I forbid you to be, you get that? Slowly I'll come over the wooden structure. Slowly. Stop whining and pull yourself together! Jesus, it's collapsing!

Where am I? That wooden sonofabitch fell under me. Why the hell not, God knows how long it's been here. What was it that the professor said, two hundred years ago? I don't know. It was an old rotten footbridge. It's much drier here than it was above. That's really weird. What was it? Did I just hear the sound of a truck going by? I did. Pull yourself together, and move forward again, slowly. Is it just me, or can I really see a light? Finally! I told you, stop being hysterical and just concentrate. Above all go slowly, so you don't step on something again. At the very end there is clearly an exit. That was a nail-biter.

Just wait, professor, you've done this on purpose! I'll show you when I get back out! He could have recognized me even with a scarf on my face. Why the hell I didn't think of this before? What if he was in the Jewish procession too? What if he turns me in? Or perhaps that old fool wanted to get rid of me straight away? Bullshit. He'd have to really loathe me.

I'm almost outside. There are bars similar to ... Well, what's that again? What? This can't be possible!

DREAM OR REALITY?

I'm hallucinating, I definitely must've gone insane. Pushing open the unlocked bars, I slowly come out of the tunnel. I'm dressed in the uniform of a Nazi officer. I don't know what rank I am, but this is simply crazy.

Down the street a group of young men is approaching, as they pull a robust black funeral car. They glimpse me and stop. Taking off their hats, they bow and say in German: "Good day, Herr Lieutenant Colonel." Then, again, they seize the car and tug and propel it forward. What's this supposed to mean? The first thing that comes to my mind is that a film is being shot here. Maybe with a hidden camera. They deliberately led me into the tunnel so I would get lost, and ... oh bullshit, what a load of ... just look around yourself, man. See the houses, they've been repaired! And those people are approaching, and there's some who are rolling on the ground... some old people.

I set off on a slow walk down the street. I sit down on a bench, I've got to breathe this out. Have I just slipped through the tunnel...to the past?! I touch my body, feeling the uniform. I've got a gun on me. I unclip the case and take out a German Luger P.08. This exact model was worn everywhere by Heinrich. A bunch of old people scuttle past, looking like beggars. They stop and bow, then they greet me in German, wishing me a nice day. "Wait, excuse me, please tell me what the date is." Did I just say that in German? I didn't used to speak German so fluently, but it seems that now I can. What's going on?! My head's reeling, I'm beginning to feel sick. Where am I, how is this possible? Jesus, I'm going to throw up. But now it's better after having just been sick in front of those old people. Silently they gaze at me. Then something can be heard from the crowd... "It's August 22nd, Herr Lieutenant Colonel."

I am a Lieutenant Colonel? Not bad: I remember they said

140

that Eichmann was a Lieutenant Colonel, and on top of that I have a skull on my cap and on the sides of my collar the golden symbols of the SS. I'm a Lieutenant Colonel of the SS, I'm in the Terezín concentration camp, and it's August 22.

"One moment, please," I stand up and I quickly catch up with the trudging crowd of dreadful looking old people.

"What year is it?" I ask them. Moon-eyed, they stare at me, then peer at each other and back at me. "1943." Nineteen forty three, I say to myself in disbelief and mutter, "Thank you."

"Can we continue, Herr Lieutenant Colonel?"

"What is it? Why, yes, continue ... continue." I return back to my bench which at this point grants me the feeling of a safe island. Have I really gone into the past? That tunnel. Again, I get queasy. My God, my brain is switching off, I feel like sleeping.

"Herr Lieutenant Colonel, wake up! Are you all right?" Someone tries to wake me up. Slowly I open my eyes, my head's still dizzy.

"Are you all right?" I hear a voice.

"Who are you?" I ask.

"I'm a nurse. The old Germans reported in the sick bay that you were sitting outside on a bench and that you weren't feeling very well. I brought a bag with medicaments. How are you feeling? What hurts you? Do you want to see a doctor? Shall I call the lift for you, Herr Lieutenant Colonel?"

"Do you know me? How do you know who I am?"

"Well, in the orders of the day it was written that the Lieutenant Colonel of the SS would be arriving to inspect the camp."

"An inspection of the camp? What the ... I don't understand, wait. Take me somewhere where I can lie down and relax, I'm not feeling well at all. Tell me, what is the date?"

"It is August 22."

"I mean the year, tell me what year."

She darts me a concerned look. "1943, of course, Herr Lieutenant Colonel. Come, I'll help you, lean on me. Just over there is the first sick bay. You can lie down there and I'll arrange a ride for you to the hospital. It's situated on the other end of town, you would not get there on foot."

"You're very kind, miss, thank you."

Wide-eyed, she peers into my eyes, and we move on. I've got my arm around hers – my whole body's trembling, I'm hardly able to lift my legs, so she supports me. Miserable, I gaze around and still can't believe what I see around me.

"Ahh, good day, Herr Obersturmbannführer, has anything happened to you?" out of the blue, an old model of a shiny brand new Volkswagen stops in front of us; I want to say a brand new model of Volkswagen. From a lowered window, with his hand hanging out, a Nazi addresses me: "Are you all right, Herr Lieutenant Colonel, sir?"

I feel bewitched. I can't seem to bring out even a single sound. I gape at him and my jaw is actually falling down. He shifts his glance over to the nurse who's holding me up and he raises his voice to her:

"What happened to him? Answer immediately, Jewess!"

"Herr Lieutenant, Herr Lieutenant Colonel was sitting on a bench and he wasn't feeling well. Old Germans reported at the sick bay that they had seen Herr Lieutenant Colonel vomiting. I took the case with medicaments right away, and ran to him."

"Oh, very well. Herr Lieutenant Colonel had a long journey; he needs rest. Help me put him into the car."

He leaves the car and helps the nurse to maneuver me into the back seat. "No no, you are coming with us, Jewess! You go nowhere, get in, you'll take care of him. He is an important guest," he snaps at the nurse. We go a few blocks, to the square. On the corner there's a modern building, Nazi flags thrust out of the windows, fluttering. They help me get out, support me, and guide me inside.

"So, these are our headquarters. I have a beautiful room with a view prepared for you. They informed me that the Lieutenant Colonel likes to appear suddenly, but I must admit I did not expect you to miss your welcoming ceremony – open-faced sandwiches, champagne, and lots of food platters were waiting for you. You had yourself dropped at the gate, did you not? You are full of surprises, Herr Lieutenant Colonel, full of surprises. And we are here, you see? A wonderful room replete with a breathtaking view of our Sudetenland and the square. We even have a little tower here – beautiful."

"I probably ate something spoiled," I suggest, as nothing else comes to mind. I stop trembling and I start to realize that what I see here is a reality. I can feel, I can hear, I can see. Unbelievably, it's unbelievably real.
I sit down on the bed, the nurse pulls down my polished knee-boots, and she slips a folded blanket under my legs.

"You will take care of Herr Lieutenant Colonel as long as he wishes! Verstanden? Did you understand?"
"Of course, Herr Lieutenant."

The Nazi leaves. The nurse comes to a sink, wets a towel and then sits down next to me and wipes my forehead.
"You are a Jewish girl, all the people here are Jewish, this is Terezín, a city of Jews. What am I doing here?" Eyeing me with a strange look, she wipes my forehead with a cold towel and smiles gently. As gentle and quiet as a sincere smile can be.

"How long have you been here? Tell me, don't worry, do not be afraid of me, I won't hurt you."
"You are so ... strange," she replies, "totally different from the

other officers I've encountered. I've been here for over a year, Herr Colonel. I'm sorry, I was mistaken, Herr Lieutenant Colonel."

"That's all right, forget it."

"All right...? Forget it? You sound so different," she smiles faintly and I notice she is blushing.

"Wait, wait, you know what? Call me Paul, please."

"But you cannot mean it. Who are you?"

"Wait, calm down. Just get ahold of yourself. If I told you, you wouldn't believe me – so I can't tell you."

"You are a Lieutenant Colonel of the SS and you want me to call you Paul? But you despise us Jews. You surely must have hurt many Jews to attain such a high rank in the SS."

"You're right, I've hurt several Jews. But they hurt me first. They took away my little girl and my dearest father. I hate them ... no, I just don't like them much. What am I saying... I don't really know."

"I'm sorry, I do not understand you."

"It doesn't matter. I'm still in shock about where I am, and I must be raving a bit. I'm so sorry. Anyway, what's your name?"

"Zdeňka. Sir, if you won't need me anymore, I will return to the first sick bay."

"No, wait, stay a bit more. Okay, go. I won't make you remain here. Run along. I'll visit you later, if I may? Thank you for your care, you've been very kind to me."

"Good bye, Herr Lieutenant Colonel."

Zdeňka closes the door behind her and the room falls quiet. A late August breeze plays with the curtains. Outside an approaching truck hums and roars, stopping in front of headquarters. I look out the window and see sloppy Nazi officers jumping from the truck. The driver and a front-seat passenger also get out. They head into the building, chatting loudly about something and laughing. A moment later, someone knocks on the door. "Next."

"Herr Lieutenant Colonel, the Camp Commander, Lieutenant Burger. Welcome to Terezín."
"At ease."
"I have heard from my assistant that you are not feeling well, Herr Lieutenant Colonel. Have you had an unpleasant journey?"

"Yes, but mainly I was celebrating for a few days, and then ate something that disagreed with me. I'm feeling much better, though perhaps I'll take another nap. Please be so kind as to leave me alone and see I'm not disturbed."

"Of course, Herr Lieutenant Colonel. By the way, the consignment is on its way, it will arrive tomorrow, the next day at the latest."

"Consignment? Well, of course – we still have time to prepare for that, right?"

"Yes, Herr Lieutenant Colonel. Would you like to view their selection and isolation? Or perhaps just examine the staff that will process them?"

I still have no idea what Burger's talking about. "Consignment", "selection" and "isolation," "processing"? About "them" – so it seems that not something, but someone is expected to arrive.

"Listen: perhaps tonight I'd like to see those who will oversee them. For now though I'll go and take a nap for a while."

"I understand, Herr Lieutenant Colonel, please inform the guard at the table. He will know where I am, and call me when you need me again." "Yes, I might have a look around myself. We'll see."

"Sieg Heil!" he slams the door and goes away. That was very

brief. Our encounter had been very awkward and I got the feeling of palpable nervousness from him. Is that why he left so quickly? Because I made him nervous? I mustn't show fear when talking to these Nazis. After all, I'm their boss.

My fluent German shocks me. In school, I had studied a little German, but I'd never been fluent like this before. So: is this really happening or not? My eyes close. I lie down on the bed. Someone will come tomorrow. Who will it be? From where? That's what I will ask those who are set up to watch them. It seems that I have a task here, I'm not here by accident: they were expecting me. So far, it doesn't make much sense. We'll see when I wake up. I can't keep my eyelids open, I'm so tired...

A roar wakes me up. Outside the Nazis are frightfully bawling someone out. People are shouting and moaning. What's going on out there?

I lean out the window. Everywhere, there are crowds of people. Behind, on the other side of the square, several motionless bodies lay on the ground. Nurses in white coats run around. I hear the wailing from passersby and people standing around. Why is it that when I first arrived the streets were almost empty, and now there are crowds? It's time to take a walk.

I wash up quickly, brush my teeth with a toothbrush that was provided, and gather my things. It's time to adapt to the situation. I'm very hungry too. Let's go explore: I mustn't forget that I'm a Lieutenant Colonel of the SS, which seems to be a very high rank. I'm getting the impression that I can do whatever I want here. Let's go see what that means in practice!

I walk through a corridor then around the supervisory table. "Heil Hitler, Herr Lieutenant Colonel! Would you like someone to accompany you, Herr Lieutenant Colonel?"

"At ease! No, that's all right, I like checking things myself. Undistracted. And tidy yourself up, man, you have a creased collar and there's a spot on your left shoe!"

"Right away, Herr Lieutenant Colonel!"

That's the way it's got to be done here, I only hark back to my military school. It was a long time ago, but I mustn't arouse suspicions. My belly rumbles. I'm come up to a little group on the other side of the square. There are police officers around, and they notice me. On the ground are the dead bodies of several old beggars. Among them lay some who are still moving and groaning. There are puddles of blood everywhere. It's a repulsive sight, it looks as if ...

"Police officer, what happened here?"

"Herr Lieutenant Colonel, perhaps it's better if you inquire at headquarters."

"Have I not told you clearly what I want to know? What happened here? Answer me now!"

"The Camp Commander here knocked down a crowd of passing old Germans. A tragic accident."

"I see, this place really reminds one of a busy road full of blind corners, right? That Herr Burger would not see them crossing the road? Hmm, strange."

A little group of nurses, together with young guys carrying stretchers, push their way through the crowd. That's the woman from yesterday, what's her name?

Yes, Zdeňka. Without hesitation, she gets busy, putting a bandage on an old man. He has an open fracture of the left hand. It's disgusting, my hunger's gone. I'd love to talk to her. Can I just pull her away from her work? There are still plenty of other nurses. One more, one less...

"Hey you, yes you, come with me!"

"But I am needed here, I have to..."

"But you do not have to. Come." Quickly, we move away from the crush of those bodies and those gruesome puddles. After a few minutes, I slow down and Zdeňka slows down with me. Silently, she stares at the ground.

"Now, let's go this way," I turn into an alley, where there are fewer people. All those who see us are bewildered, and stop to gape at us. They bow and greet me, yet they also watch Zdeňka with a look full of fear and worry.

"Do you know what happened in the square?"
"Yes."
"So tell me. You don't have to be afraid, I won't say anything to anybody. That police officer back there didn't want to tell me. He was afraid of me, or he feared Burger, I don't know."
"The Camp Commander occasionally entertains himself by driving a truck through a crowd of people, mostly the elderly. They are slow, and have poor hearing and eyesight, and do not manage to jump aside. By the time they notice the truck coming, it's too late."
Hmm. so that's what it looks like when someone can do whatever he or she wants. I can also do anything I want; it's just that I'd never think to run over a crowd.
"What else does the Camp Commander do here?"
"Herr Lieutenant Colonel, I cannot talk about it, forgive me. Can I go back to work?"
"No, you cannot! Answer me immediately, or ...!"
Zdeňka looks at me with horror, eyes equally appalled and reproaching me. But then she remembers her place, and bends her head and utters softly:
"Sometimes he shoots someone on the sidewalk because they did not hear his greeting and reply. People are disappearing. At night, they silently burst into girls' quarters and some of them are taken to headquarters. Only a few return. Those who do...

148

are always somehow disfigured, but they don't say a word about what happened. Then they are sent away with the next transport for camps in the East."

"Come: show me exactly where you live and where you work. Where is it? Take me there."
"We have to go back, this way."
"Everywhere there are so many people; how can you find any privacy here?" I ask.

"That's because they've just returned from work. Now they have two and a half hours to visit each other. Husbands with their wives, and children with their parents. They have brought something they saved from lunch for them. At half past nine is the counting and the curfew starts at nine: everyone must be inside the barracks or in their block."

"Why are so many old people lying around, they stink terribly. Why doesn't anyone help them, they don't have a family here?"
"Those old ones from the Reich, they don't have anyone here."
"But the people step over them, as if they weren't even there."
"Nobody can do anything to help them. They live in rooms underground, and inside the walls."

"What did you say? In the walls?"
"Yes, in the walls there are loads of rooms and tunnels. They began arriving a year ago and there were no rooms to them in. The city is full of our countrymen, Czech Jews, entire families. I do not know why they send them from the Reich to a Czech Jewish city. Certainly, that is something you must know."
"Heil Hitler, Herr Lieutenant Colonel! I can see you took a fancy to your nurse. Yes, she's a handy little Jewish bitch, isn't she?"

All of a sudden, the Deputy Commander of the camp emerges from behind a corner. I forgot his name, the one from the Volkswagen. Did he even tell me? With a salacious, perverse look, he eyes Zdeňka:

"I have finally found you, Herr Lieutenant Colonel. They told me that you went for a walk. Lieutenant Burger sent me to tell you that a gala dinner starts in your honor to be followed by a small banquet in the officers' club. There will be lots of beautiful Sudeten girls, you understand."

"Yes, thank you, you can go. Leave us..."

"I understand, sir. Heil Hitler!"

He leaves, but before that he strangely runs his eyes over Zdeňka one more time. I don't have a good feeling about this; I don't want to cause her trouble. She told me many things that I wouldn't learn otherwise. The feeling I've gotten is she's a good, gentle girl, with a kindly soul.

"Right. Thank you for clarifying my stomach problems. Bring the pills for me to headquarters tomorrow morning. I do not need you anymore – go back to work. Heil Hitler!" Well, I don't have to add it, but I'm sure that Burger's assistant overheard my words. With her high-pitched voice, this polite nurse reminds me of someone, as if I knew her from somewhere else. It's a voice I've certainly heard somewhere before. I'll return to headquarters – I need to obtain a clean uniform, have my shoes polished, and take a shower. Regarding food, I'll wait till supper time to eat properly. I get the impression it's not going to be so bad here and think I can get used to this environment. It's fascinating to be back in nineteen fortythree. How could things have changed to become so ... exciting?

"Heil Hitler, Herr Obersturmbannführer! So how do you feel now, are you better?" Camp Commander Burger addresses me right at the entrance to the hall.

"Heil Hitler! Yes, I feel much better, thank you."

A guard has just led me to a small room within the headquarters. There are loads of Nazis here, along their wives and various other young women. They speak German and also Czech. Most likely, they're from the area. The wait staff wear armbands with stars. There are more of them than I expected. Youngish Jewish girls hand out champagne and carry platters of open-faced sandwiches and desserts. I stop one of them and take a glass from her.

"Burger, please fill me in on the details of the consignment that should arrive tomorrow."

"What do you mean, Herr Lieutenant Colonel? How is it you don't know who's coming, and why? Now that's really strange. Can't you remember why you are here?"

So, this is not the way to ask. He'll immediately get suspicious and find out that I don't know anything about it. But how can I go about obtaining the information I need? What kind of consignment is in question? It's sure to be something important, and that's why they've sent me to oversee it. I've got to be very careful.

"You mentioned the doctors and nurses that you want to show me. Where are they? Do you have them ready?"

"Ah ... well, of course, I almost forgot. My sincere apologies, Herr Lieutenant Colonel. I'll have it arranged right away: within fifteen minutes they will be ready. Actually, I thought that you would want to enjoy yourself with the local Czech German women, but I see that Herr Lieutenant Colonel is working constantly. I will be right back, Heil Hitler!"

I think I handled this well, I reach into a chair. I mustn't forget who I am. It's all right to remain distant from the others. Not to venture into any unnecessary talk with anyone. I don't have to. I've come because of an important task, although I don't know what it is, but soon I'm going to find out. In the hall, people slowly start to take notice of me. I admit that it's not overly pleasant. Nobody wants to talk to me. Well, speak of the devil, and... "Heil Hitler, Herr Lieutenant Colonel! Come and make a toast with us. I would like to introduce you to my lady and her friends – they like you very much," Burger's representative invites me to meet them. That's just what I need. Do I have to go? In my thoughts I swear, but aloud I say: "Well, only because it is you. I have a head full of work and I am still not feeling at my best. So, just for a moment."

"I understand, Herr Lieutenant Colonel, it is a great honor for me, thank you."
Introductions are in order and then chitchat about the weather. Just at the moment when they get around to questions of how the Führer is doing and what it's like to spend time so close to him, Burger comes to let me know that everything is ready: they are all lined up in the building next door, a Jewish cafe.
"Yes, very good. Excuse me – work calls. Heil Hitler!"
"Heil Hitler, Herr Lieutenant Colonel!"

We go out to the square, and walk to the adjacent building. There's complete silence everywhere, no one is to be seen anywhere.
"Where are all the Jews, Burger? During the day, there were thousands of them."

"After nine o'clock they all have to be back in their homes, Herr Lieutenant Colonel, and they may go outside only with a special permit. In the winter, they can only be out until eight, and after ten the lights must be turned off everywhere, no matter if it is summer or winter. Simply, after ten it must be dark. And here we are. This way, please."

We enter a room that serves as a Jewish cafe. I'm told that during the day only those Jews who have a special ticket may enter, and that it is apparently very expensive; a place for the

Jewish upper class.

"So, here we have them, Herr Lieutenant Colonel. All 53 of them. In this line there are doctors, over here nurses ... and here are some teachers. As you can see, the majority of them are women. You know, they are better suited for little children. And also, God knows in what condition they will arrive. It's quite a distance from Białystok, and now with those problems on the Eastern front, in many places they have to wait at the station until our supplies are searched. But everything is ready, on the outskirts of the city, the single story wooden houses have been built and the barbed wire fence is completed. No one can get to them from inside the city, complete isolation, of course, protected by a special guard unit of the Small Fortress. Yes, people from Jöckel. Czech gendarmes can be trusted, after all, as can the Jewish guards – those loyal toadies will do anything we ask to help us for a bit more bread, but it's better to be safe than sorry." Burger, who's already had a lot to drink, laughs. They stand at attention and do not utter a sound. Apparently, they're very afraid of Burger. No wonder; for from what little I've heard about him, he must be a sadist. So, children from Białystok? I have no idea where that is. It sounds like a Russian city, or perhaps a Polish one? Why should they come here? And why in poor condition? And how many of them will there be? Slowly, I walk around the lines, thinking what to ask so as not to reveal myself. Burger stares at me, waiting for what's going to come out of me.

"Good work, Burger. Now what do we do with them?"
"They will take them to the isolation area, settle them in, and get ready for tomorrow. Now that they have heard our conversation, they will not go back among their own people. Therefore, the bags are all here: they have things for two months; perhaps negotiations will not take longer. There's no

need to worry: of course we already searched them quite thoroughly."

Negotiations ... children from Białystok ... isolation ... doctors ... What does it all mean? Bring children here, take them into isolation, they can't be among others. Do they know something? The caretakers will also be locked up with them for two months. Why can't they come here from their homes? The children might tell them something that no one is meant to find out. We'll see tomorrow ...

"That is enough for me, Burger, thank you, have them taken away. I'll take a little stroll through your Terezín. I have a head full of ideas. Heil Hitler!"

I think that at least for now I've managed to make the right impression. Burger gives the order to a guard and the crowd of doctors, nurses and caregivers with their large bags set off in a quiet and orderly motion. But what's going on is still gnawing at the back of my mind: "Wait, Burger! The situation in Białystok was very bad, I know, but why isolation? Do you think these kids are so dangerous? Why not integrate them for a while with the others? Why must the numbers of guards in the Small Fortress be reduced because of a few dozen children? Are they so ferocious?" I wink at him.

"Naturally, I understand where Herr Lieutenant Colonel is heading with this, but there is no need to worry. Yesterday, reinforcements arrived from the elite SS units. We will soon get rid of the Jewish police. There are 250 of them here, 250 of our little helpers. In Jewish Białystok they were the ones who, in fact, started their desperate comic revolution. They were very well organized and it took three days until our men finally shot all of them down. The children saw it all; they also know about the gas chambers. They know from their dead parents what the family camp at Birkenau means. And we cannot afford to let the local Jews learn this. You understand me, Herr Lieutenant Colonel."

"Of course, it would wreak havoc with all our plans, but tell me, Burger, how did those in Białystok learn about what is really going on in Birkenau?" Although the room is already empty, Burger lowers his voice:

"The truth, but you do not have it from me, Herr Lieutenant Colonel, is that an SS unit that was in charge of the Białystok ghetto conspired with the local Jews. People were either running away or else getting the information inside, so sooner or later they had to learn what is happening on the other side of Poland. They knew about the gas chambers; they knew where their whole families ended up. They thought that they could stop it, poor things." Burger resumes his cackling laughter. To cover my consternation, I laugh as well. Now at last it's clear what's going on. I'll put the whole thing together again, but only outside, before we get into a deeper conversation. I have to get out!

"Well, I'm going for a walk. See you later. Heil Hitler!" I say goodbye. "Heil Hitler, Herr Lieutenant Colonel!"

Silence is everywhere, from the window I occasionally hear a wailing that seems to come out of nowhere; the streets are, with only a few exceptions, empty. Sometimes a group of men or women passes by. I'm slowly heading back towards the tunnel through which I came to this place. It's not hard to find your way around here, all the streets lined with rightangled buildings are organized in blocks, and between them are tremendously long barracks. No matter which direction you walk, you end up at the ramparts, walls, or entrances to the tunnels in the walls. Every now and then I meet some gendarmes on nighttime guard duty, and occasionally, a car with Nazi officers passes by. The sound of music from the banquet, which I successfully withdrew from, is slowly fading as I walk through a grim, empty street. I approach the ramparts. It was here somewhere.

"Good evening, Herr Lieutenant Colonel," another Czech policeman on patrol greets me.

"Good evening. Tell me, are you not afraid that someone will slip and simply get lost in the tunnels or that he or she will quietly disappear under the cover of night? It could not be that hard to escape."

"The Jews would not dare, Herr Lieutenant Colonel. You know, to run away from here would not be that difficult, but to survive out there is impossible, and they know that very well. Also, to run away means leaving with the whole family, Herr Lieutenant Colonel. If they should leave someone behind, I mean anyone from the family, that member would be condemned to death for it. In the morning, there is a roll call, and there's counting three times during the day – at home, at work, in the hospital.

Everyone knows their place, where they go to be counted. If they are late, even by a few minutes, they're considered to be fugitives. Mostly, even though they finally do show up, they are still taken up to headquarters, and then to the Small Fortress. And from there nobody returns, Herr Lieutenant Colonel."

"Naturally. It's just that it seems to me that this place is not so well guarded. After all, look over there. Who is guarding the trenches between the walls?"

"All around there are swamps, and everyone around here knows that out there no one will help a Jew. On the contrary:

anyone who would help a Jew to escape or conceal that they saw a fugitive would be executed, along with their whole family, you know? This place is better guarded by the surrounding population than by guards inside."

"Hmm, interesting. Carry on with your activities, officer. I will not disturb you any longer."

"I understand, Herr Lieutenant Colonel."

Now it's clear to me, very clear. This Small Fortress is a very interesting place, but the devil takes it. I have to start considering why I'm here. Or perhaps, how to get out of here again. Was it some sort of a time tunnel that led me here? Why 1943, and not some other time, like when this place was built during Habsburg's reign? And anyway, what does it look like outside? Can I just take a trip to Prague to a cafe, like the one in the Municipal House or Wenceslas Square? What is going on with my head? And I'm beginning to miss my little Maria. I've been away for two days already, and the place where I regularly hide in the bushes to watch her must be empty. I haven't seen her for two whole days! Also, Kurt and Heinrich will be looking for me, or at least I hope so. They mentioned a new contract for loads of money, and honestly, I need it. How long am I going to be here? I'm starting to lose my nerve. I've got to explore the tunnel; my answer lies there.

Here it is: the bars are locked – but what was I expecting? A sign on the entrance with an arrow pointing 'Back to the Future'? Wait, where's a police officer or a guard? They must be here somewhere.

"Officer, I need keys to the bars over there. Where can I get it? Is there a superintendent, or are the keys hanging somewhere?"

"Unfortunately not, Herr Lieutenant Colonel. For these bars, only I have the keys, at the back, this is my beat. In the morning we hand over the keys to the next shift."

"Come with me, I need to unlock it. I wonder where it leads and what is inside. You have a flashlight, right?"

"I understand, Herr Lieutenant Colonel, yes, I have a flashlight, of course." The officer is nervous as unlocks the gate, I notice. What's going on here? You, buddy, will know much more, so you'd better come along with me. "Officer, you will walk in front of me and shine the light on our path. Where is this going?"

"Herr Lieutenant Colonel, this tunnel does not really lead anywhere. All the intersections are bricked up."

"All right, we will see then. Continue. What are you waiting for? Go!"

Slowly we approach the first junction with other tunnels.

"But it seems that not all of the paths are bricked up, doesn't it? After all, this tunnel continues!"

"Yes, but at the next intersection it will all be walled up, Herr Lieutenant Colonel, truly."

"Where did these tunnels lead: speak, man!" The officer is visibly more and more ill at ease. As we continue through the long cold tunnel to that last walled intersection, his agitation increases. As if he knew about the tunnel of time? Oh, bollocks! But what if? What if I climb back to my time, to 2002? I can hear something up ahead.

"What was that? Did you hear that? Bricks, I heard bricks. Come on, hurry up!" The officer doesn't feel like running. What's really going on here? Finally, we run up to a crossroads. I take the flashlight from the frightened policeman, carefully looking through the walled entrances. I've got it! Here it is. In one entrance, there's a hole and someone is behind the wall. He was laying bricks and one had to fall down and hit the other. That was the sound I heard. I pull out a pistol and point it at the officer.

"Give me your gun and rifle, come on!" Slowly he hands the smaller weapon over, giving me a mistrustful look. I take the rifle from his shoulder myself.

"Now kick it real hard!"

Adrenalin suddenly springs to my blood, my jaw clenches and I'm ready for anything. The officer kicks in the wall. Bricks fall off and on the other side we see faces of young men. There are three of them. Along with the officer that makes four people I can take down in a few seconds if they try any tricks on me.

"Switch on the flashlight! Yes, you! And I can see you've got one as well. So turn it on, and put your hands up! No! Only the hand that you're holding the light with. Now, you'll do lamps, aim the lights down. When your hand hurts you tell me and you can slowly change hands. Do you understand me?" Everyone's scared and tense. Slowly, they're glancing at each other. Like that, guys. Don't make me shoot you.

"Don't even think of trying something. None of you make a hasty move; I'll shoot you faster than you say 'Jew', right?" And then one of them starts:

"You think you are strong, but that's only because you have weapons. It is easy to lord it over the weak ones."

"What? You've got courage, man, to speak to me like that. What's your name?"

"Jakob," he proudly straightens up and continues his lecture, "the only thing you can do is to shoot me, but you can never break us. Truly strong is the one who does not pull out a gun before the weak one on his knees. Strong is he who has mercy."

Tears trickle down his cheek; he's shaking, determined to die. We have a night session underground. They have no idea who I am and are waiting for me to shoot them all. I'm just not

... or am I? No, I'm not who this desperate group thinks I am. I couldn't kill anyone; I'm just protecting those who play at being Nazis because they belong nowhere else in society. They pay well and set fire to the walls of the synagogue. But what does it matter? After a while the gasoline evaporates and the fire is extinguished, so it's just a black form of comedy. Oh, but hold on, buddy: you're forgetting the poor ones you knocked out on the street? You aren't innocent – far from it. But this right here is the reality, the real Nazis here have real power to kill when they please, and Jews here think I'm one of those.

"Truly strong is the one who bears his own fate, even if it is death. We know what you do with us in the East. We know you're murdering women and children by the hundreds. What sort of heroism is that? You have power over half of the world, but have you changed anything for good? You only spread disaster and death with pride and cruelty. Blindly and faithfully, you serve the devil. You are forgetting that storms never last forever, and one day a pure light will reach you, shining even into the darkest corner. And that pride comes before a heavy fall. The day will come when you will be held accountable for your actions, sir. Then, look around you, if you'll see bravery. You'll see if you'll proudly bear the consequences of your madness."

"Have you finished? Yes? You, Mr. Speechmaker, untie them." The Czech policeman starts to cry. Nobody knows what will happen next. What I will do to them. The speaker unties the last bag and tugs out bread, plates and cigarettes. And toys? They are smuggling toys in with the food? What's that supposed to mean?

"Put it back. Now, everyone, we'll move through the tunnel to the place where you were taking those bags. Walk ahead of me!"

We are slowly approaching a narrowing tunnel hole in the wall. Slowly, one by one, they climb inside. On the other side of the hole, a huge old wardrobe is shoved aside. We slip into a basement room.

"Somewhere here there must be switch, turn the lights on!"

Let there be light. What I see takes my breath away: little children are crowded onto the three-story bunk beds constructed along the wall. Around fifty or perhaps even sixty of them are huddled together, jostling for room. On each bed floor there are two or three toddlers. They are emaciated, disheveled and dirty. We all look at each other. For a moment there, time just stops. We are all silent, my knees give way and I have to sit down on the bench. I thought I had caught smugglers with weapons, or traffickers who earn money in Terezín's black market, big money, but this, this I was not expecting.

"What will you do with us, sir?"

I am silent; I do not want them to see how my chin is shaking, how tears have started to well at the corners of my eyes from all of this.

"Don't worry; I will say nothing of this. I do not belong here, any more than you do. Goodbye. You have to watch out better next time and don't get taken by surprise."

I take off the rifle and return it with the pistol to the policeman. I take the flashlight and pull myself through a hole in the wall just in time before I start to cry. I go back down that long dark tunnel, back to the entrance, when the young speaker catches up with me.

"Sir, Lieutenant Colonel, what you just did was marvelous. Are you crying? For God's sake, who are you?"

Again, I stagger and I have to sit on one of the stones near the entrance. "Are you all right sir, Lieutenant Colonel, who are you?"

"I would like to be with my little one, I miss her. I don't know if I'll ever see her again."

"And where is your home sir?"

"My home? In Prague. Well, this is how it really is ... in Prague in 2002, Jakob. 2002. God, what am I saying? Forget it, my head hurts and I'm still so exhausted."

Jakob stares at me with a frightened look; now he definitely must think I'm a mental case. Pull yourself together, stand on your feet, and then go back to my room to sleep. You can do it, so what are you waiting for? I can't, I'm so weak. Now, chills also reach me, I start to shake. I'm in 1943, for God's sake, how is this possible? I am in 1943. Eyes close, breathing slows.

"Herr Lieutenant Colonel, wake up!"

"Where am I? What happened?" I open my eyes; to find I'm lying on the ground floor of a bunk bed. Around me sit dirty little children. I'm back in that room.

"You've got me here ..."

"Yes, I ran for help with the police officer and with the help of others we carried you here. You passed out, Herr Lieutenant Colonel."

"Stop it with the 'Lieutenant Colonel'. Thank you, Jakob. Since the time I've been here, I have a terrible headache – it just comes out of nowhere, and I'm not myself at all."

"Relax."

A small boy of about five years old gives me a glass of water, another little girl brings a wrapped wet towel and places it on my forehead.

"Where have the policeman and the others gone? Can you tell me?" "Herr Lieutenant Colonel, don't worry. The officer had to go back to his position. Someone might notice that he is missing in his area. Now you do not meet Nazis in Terezín so often at night, but there's no doubt he is where he should be. Others quietly returned to their quarters. They hope that you will not inform on us."

"I told you I don't belong here. I think I know why I'm here. I'm not a good man, Jakob. I have worked for very evil people and somehow it happened that I've been sent back in time to understand it. And just me! Why not them?"

"I do not understand you at all, Herr Lieutenant Colonel. I am so sorry about that. I would like to understand you, but what we just went through and heard from you doesn't make any sense."

I notice how the kids are falling asleep. Huddling next to one another, now they don't have any worries, quietly sleeping. Jakob, this young Jewish guy, wears a naive expression on his face but he's clearly full of determination.

"I know, Jakob, I'm glad I've met you. How old are you?"
"Nineteen, Herr Lieutenant Colonel."

"Cut it out with the Colonel crap, please. Call me Paul, it must be clear by now that I'm no Lieutenant Colonel. Tell me, why are these kids not with the others? Why are they sleeping here in a hidden basement?"

"They live here; they are children of the orphanage. A month ago they were supposed to go to Auschwitz, but we in the resistance know about the mass murders there, so we made them dead on paper. We have our people protected – and now we have to hide them here."

"How can I help you, Jakob? Please think of something, will you? Where can I find you throughout the day?"
"Sir, I still cannot believe it. But you can find me in the workshops of the old Germans, in the department for painters and artists."

"Artists, you say?"

163

"Yes, I'm a poet and a painter."

"I noticed that in your speech. Mainly, you're very brave, Jakob. Soon I'll seek you out and you, along with the others, prepare a plan. Agreed?" "Agreed ... Paul."

It took a while before I got back to headquarters. I walked slowly, thinking about everything. The whole city was plunged into sleep. I walked past the Nazis sleeping at the table and finally I lay down in my room, hoping that everything here has just been an incredible and confused dream.

A squeal of locomotive brakes making a long train of wagons shriek to a stop wakes me up. Maybe the Białystok transport's arrived? So soon? It's half past eight – I must have slept well. I think maybe I didn't even dream during the night. A pleasant deep sleep in 1943. Yesterday I didn't find the tunnel, but instead met a few men from the local resistance and Jakob, the brave young poet, or rather speaker. I must visit him later. But what time did he say?

"Herr Lieutenant Colonel, are you awake? Can I come in?"

"One moment!" Well. Burger. Don't forget that you're the boss here. Everyone's afraid of you. You can exactly as you please with them. These words have got to become a mantra for me. Where are my pants! Why are you in a hurry? That fellow will just have to wait, he's got to. So, pretty calm, and with an arrogant tone I call to him.

"Come in!"

"Good morning, Herr Lieutenant Colonel! I hope that you are sleeping well here in Terezín. Personally, I sleep badly just before the transports. You know, it's always bedlam when they arrive. Sorry, I know that you have a reputation as a loner and that you in no time and place wish to be disturbed, but still: I wanted to inform you that the consignment will arrive around two in the afternoon."

"Wait, Burger. I heard the arrival of locomotives and wagons just moments ago."

"Not at all, Herr Lieutenant Colonel. It's only a train that arrived to take the locals to Auschwitz, and in a half hour another one comes. This is for family members of locals; the prominent ones say. It will deliver a hundred of our little Jews to the Reich. Fresh young girls are needed there to manufacture uniforms. Two transports and we have five hundred units, nothing special – just a minor affair, really. Once we had a departure of three thousand in one day, which is what we in Vienna call a real bedlam."

"In Vienna you say? I have been there several times. Belvedere is magnificent and I'd be able to spend even the whole day in Schönbrunn." What are you blathering on about again? Don't allow yourself by any means to settle into a deeper conversation. I have to lead it out to nowhere. "Schönbrunn Palace? Well of course. I forgot a man in your position even gets into the family of the former emperor. How wonderful: certainly you have had many enviable experiences, Herr Lieutenant Colonel, and if you find the time tonight to join our party in the officers' club..."

Yeah – that was close. Have you forgotten that it's probably not yet a museum open to the public? Just as well I'm a colonel of the SS. Don't yak with this Nazi – just send him back out the door!

"Actually, I do not know how I will feel tonight after such a significant day as today. You know what: tell someone to bring my breakfast in here! Scrambled eggs, lightly browned bread on both sides, jam, butter, salami, pate, sausages, strong coffee, milk."

"Sorry? Of course, I understand, Herr Lieutenant Colonel. I understand, if you need anything, the car is always ready in front of the house, just give the command to a guard and he'll take care of everything. I am going to supervise the transport; I will not take up any more of your time. Heil Hitler, Herr Lieutenant Colonel!"

I really enjoy my breakfast. That goose pate from the Litoměřice butcher, Steiner, according to the label on the glass, was simply terrific. And that bread and salami! People from my time have no idea what a proper pate or a sausage without preservatives tastes like. Such delicacies! What happened to food over the years? I think I'll go visit Zdeňka. Perhaps I should apologize to her; the last time we met I wasn't nice to her at all.

I set out from the headquarters and turn straight right. I pass the Jewish cafe; go by shops with household goods, cross the road and along the block where Jewish girls are housed. I continue at a slow, leisurely pace straight toward the hospital gate. Along the way I again see the impoverished old people lying around on the pavement, and even on the road. And in other places, the elders beg at the windows. Around me are crowds of Jews rushing to their homes and maybe even to work. I stop and watch the hustle and bustle of people who are moving from one place to somewhere else. The old ones aren't even noticed by anyone. A young man even stepped over an old woman lying on the street as he walked by. I don't understand: I don't quite know what's happening here. Other people are decently dressed, even the laborers or young women, and a few of the old ladies too. A small group of children walk by with their tutor and they beautifully smarten themselves up. Everybody is pretty much all right, except for these poor old people who stink, beg, and roll on the ground. I'll ask Zdeňka about this. I'm curious what she'll say. Who are these old ones that no one even notices?

"Good morning, doctor, sir. I am looking for Miss Zdeňka: she works on the first sick bay. Today she should have a shift here in the hospital. Where can I find her?"

"Good morning, Herr Lieutenant Colonel! Of course, she was working here until this morning. She is departing as an assistant to the family camp in the East right now. And now if you will excuse me, I have to attend to the patients."

What? She's departing to the East? She would have mentioned this, but then again, I'm a Lieutenant Colonel of the SS and she was afraid of me, just like everyone else. Why would she bother to say goodbye?

"Excuse me, doctor. Didn't she leave a note? We agreed that she would help me with something."

"Sorry? A note? She has certainly not left one here. In the early morning she was brought in along with a few of her friends on a stretcher. She barely crawled back to her home. They were tortured at the headquarters in the basement along with five other girls. Now if you'll excuse me." "Wait, damn it! Who tortured her? What happened to her? Speak, man!" "The Camp Commander sometimes picks up a few Jewish girls at midnight, mostly before the departure of one of the transports. It is certain that no one knows about what they did: no one. Those few girls that were brought here together with others were assigned to the transport. And I guess at any moment they will come for me, too."

"Burger?"

"With all due respect, Herr Lieutenant Colonel, are you not, as an inspector, supposed to know everything?"

That bastard Burger! I knew when his representative met us on the
street, it wouldn't turn out well for her later. That look of his foreboded trouble. They kidnap the girls at night and torture

167

them? What perversion is this?

"Did they rape her?"

"Not the way you think, Herr Lieutenant Colonel, no. They use a variety of batons and sticks. Otherwise they would not dare. Someone could report them for intercourse with a Jewish girl. They take turns burning them, everyone on a different part of the body. They burned Zdeňka's whole shoulder, from the collarbone to the neck. Basically they mutilated and disfigured it. And now, if you will really excuse me, after this conversation ... I am going to pack my things."

"From the shoulder through the collarbone up to the neck? What are you saying? It cannot be... Doctor, what is Zdeňka's last name?"

"Sorry? You want to know the surname of a Jew? An SS Lieutenant Colonel?"

"Look here, doctor, you're starting to wind me up, and if you continue then tomorrow you'll admire the sunrise through the wagon hole where it really rises. Yes, me, I want to know the surname of that Jew, at once!" Terrified, he's staring at me over his glasses. From his resigned look, which had seen more than I would've imagined before the war, there's a good deal of surprise to be seen.

"Doctor! Her surname!"

"That unfortunate girl's called Zdeňka Rabbová. Zdeňka Rabbová."

That's just not possible. I was ten years old. That burn mark. That surname. It can't be. It was me who ... God, then in the living room during the family gathering, when all the children were taken to the children's room, I didn't understand a word, what she was screaming hysterically to my aunt and uncles. My God, she was shouting:

"Jews. You Janny, you Milan, Julia, Pauli, we are all Jews."

My head's dizzy ... Quick! My God! I've got to save her! "Doctor, call! Call immediately!"

I start to panic every time something I really care about is at stake. Every time, I sink into a momentary whirlpool of anxiety and utter panic. It's necessary to breathe smoothly, to calm down. The doctor leads me to an office with a telephone. It shows the highlighted numbers that can be called, but there's not an outside line. 01's the headquarters. Remember that you are the Lieutenant Colonel of the SS. You can do absolutely anything! Once again: you can do anything. Never stop repeating this.

"Hello, this is the Lieutenant Colonel of the SS, stop the transport immediately! The transport cannot leave without my consent; do you understand me? It must not leave!" I throw away the handset and I start to run. Within seconds, I'm down at the end of the hall. I take perhaps ten stairs at once. I rush out of the main hospital courtyard. Frantically, I look around. There are no cars anywhere. I look for an ambulance, but one is nowhere to be found. I might as well have given orders to send a car to the bloody hospital. There's nothing to be done. This will have to be a sprint. I set out across a little square and arrive at the hospital gate. The guard opens the door for me, so I can run out onto the street. In my haste

I collide with a crowd of marching men and knock down a few of them. They help me back on my feet, and bow to me. I race like a madman along the houses up to the square. Crowds around me are stopping to stare. Policemen, moon-eyed, salute me. In front of the headquarters, mills a crowd of Nazis. "Heil Hitler!" they greet me. I yell at them to unlock the car.

"Immediately to the station. Come on, go!" The startled sergeant steps hard on the pedal. "I need you to stop before the train engine!"

169

We drive about two blocks and in a few minutes we're there. At the last minute, the wagons are already boarded up. The platform alongside the train is empty. They're all inside. Wherever one looks, there are SS guards stationed. Czech gendarmes and Jewish police, all of whom now turn their gaze to me. From a distance, Burger, in a dynamic stride, approaches me with several other officers. I set out towards him with a vigorous step. Don't forget who you are. There must be respect oozing out of every pore, so get busy. And resolutely...

"At once, summon Rabbová, my personal nurse, to me! Find Rabbová and remove her from this train. That's an order, Burger! Find her immediately!"

"Herr Lieutenant Colonel, you cannot. This is against all the rules."

"Leave us alone." I take Burger aside, lower my voice, and whisper to him: "I know about your torture games, Burger. I know all about what you do, absolutely without supervision. Your whole operation here is against the rules. Do you understand me? If you do not wish to be sent to the Eastern front immediately, find Rabbová with no tricks and no delays. Then load her onto a working unit transport to Germany. Right now. Do you understand me, Burger? Tell me that you understand!" Burger's in shock, he's all flushed. "I understood you, Herr Lieutenant Colonel. Raabováá! Find me Ráábbovááá!"

The Jewish police are now circling around each wagon. Everyone screams the name Rabbová, and finally from one coach, a voice says "Here she is, here." The SS men break the seal that locks the sliding doors. I stand by the car and quietly observe everything. It's busy at the open wagon. One of the Jewish policemen runs into the building and, after a while, returns with a stretcher. Zdeňka can't even walk, after the way the Nazis have battered her last night. They bring her from the cattle car and head to another nearby trailer where the train for civilians is parked, a train to a female labor camp in Germany, out of which they don't send anyone East. The Nazis open the gates. Again, they lock it and seal it. All because of a single Jewish girl. No one utters a word of protest. No one asks any questions. I hold my hands behind my back and stand confidently upright. The stretcher with Zdeňka is brought around me. She looks at me as she passes by. I look at her. And now time slows down again. We're passing by one another and our gaze seems to encompass an eternity of knowing. She's slowly closing her lid: she wants me to know that she knew that it was me who had her pulled out of the transports to the East.

If only you knew, Zdeňka, precisely who you'll be telling this story to in forty years. You'll have a long and beautiful life, many children ... and your first son ... will be my father. One day, the cute little boy whose look reminds you of someone in the past; it'll be me – Grandma.

The whistle blows and the train rocks into motion. Within a few minutes, it disappears altogether behind the walls of the former fortress. A few minutes later, even the train with a few cars, for civilians, sets off. I stand by the car, my hands behind my back and I look at this one also slowly disappearing from sight. The policemen are dispersing. The Jewish guards go to attend to their other business. The Nazis get on their motorcycles with sidecars and slowly depart to the Small Fortress, others only two blocks away, to the headquarters on the square. The city is once again filled with the hot August silence. I take a walk after sending the driver away. He gave me the cigarette I asked for before he left: I need to smoke. He heil-hitlers me and leaves.

So. That was the reason I'm here. I met my grandmother when she was nineteen years old. This was bound to happen: she told me about it when I was a boy. She said that not all Nazis were evil. That the man who saved her life was completely different. You were wrong about something there, Grandma. The one who saved your life wasn't a Nazi then and he never will be again.

"Herr Obersturmbannführer, I have a message for you from the Camp Commander, Lieutenant Burger. The consignment will be delayed, arriving in the evening. Herr Lieutenant asks you if you'll join him for lunch in half an hour at the officers' club."

A Volkswagen's arrival interrupts my moment of peace in a park next to the Hannover barracks. I was thinking once again about what this strange journey actually wanted to tell me. Perhaps I've already understood which side I belong to. I smile at the fact that the bodyguard of one of the prominent leaders of the neo-Nazi leadership is a half-Jew, and I'm thinking about how this all began. What made me into someone who protects those beasts? Those who long to be someone who wields absolute power over the life and death of innocent others have rarely understood their own pasts. But how could I understand such an extreme? Yet my fate had somehow led me to nineteen forty-three, so I'd start thinking and rescue my own grandmother? What am I supposed to do now – how does this work? Do I just go back to sleep and wake up at home? After all this I feel this bench on which I'm sitting, I can taste the tart tobacco of the cigarette lent by the guard. This is actually no dream ...

"First, tell me what's going to be for lunch," I reply.
"I do not know, Herr Lieutenant Colonel, but certainly several courses that even Herr Lieutenant Colonel can choose from.

What should I tell Herr Commander Burger?"

"All right, all right. Of course I'll join him for lunch. Go, I will arrive later. Tell him that I am coming in half an hour."

"I understand, Herr Lieutenant Colonel, Heil Hitler!"

Well guys, about all that proud heil-hitlering: if only you knew how it's going to turn out with your dear Hitler! What are you doing? Don't yield here, man. Do you want them to start to get suspicious? Do you want everyone to realize that you're no Nazi, not to mention no Lieutenant Colonel of the SS? You'd better greet him back the right way before you get into trouble, man. Well, come on, go right ahead!

"Heil Hitler!"

I stroll around and try to prepare for a conversation with the sadist Burger. Certainly it'll take some preparation.

"And here, our dear Herr Lieutenant Colonel. We are waiting just for you, take a seat please." Come on, buddy, don't forget who you are. Straighten up and be serious and aloof: it's important to adopt and maintain a standoffish persona.

"Herr Untersturmführer, what time do we expect the arrival of the next consignment? I hope it will be in order," I deploy a distant tone.

"I know, Herr Lieutenant Colonel, you have to worry about many issues, traveling from camp to camp and making inspections. Let me explain to you a few facts about the transport we are waiting for."

"Exactly, Herr Burger. Finally, someone understands me. My head is awhirl from all those visits. I will probably need a vacation, as soon as possible." Burger starts to smile. I feel he's pleased that I let him closer. He starts eating the soup they've just brought in; and the others do as well. Around the oblong table are sitting eight noncommissioned SS officers with ranks lower than Burger's. None of them even dares to utter a sound. When our eyes meet, they smile and lower their eyes. That's fine; just no questions, no interviews.

"You know where I would go? To Greece – beautiful women there, wonderful food, the sun, and the beach. Even though we still have some problems with the resistance in the mountains, it is my dream destination. A few years ago, I showed them how to handle the locals. Sorry, I got a little carried away. So: this exceptional consignment is of great value for us, you surely know that – you know Herr Eichmann as I do – so I do not need to mention to you the negotiations by his assistant Wysliceny with representatives of the Red Cross and the governments. But what you certainly do not know, Herr Inspector, is that here in Terezín nobody can even get close to them, because the little Jewish brats already know about Birkenau."

"You already told me this when I came to look over the staff who will take care of them. They have also witnessed the murders in Białystok. Surely you will be keeping an eye on maintaining solid isolation."

"Oh, of course, Herr Inspector, they will still be watched by the SS guards, what else? No one will even come close to them. By the way, Herr Lieutenant Colonel, could we here at Terezín also count on a promotion, if this business comes off according to plan, and we get back those prisoners of ours and perhaps even some money to defray our expenses?"

"I think so. You know everything, man. I assumed that Berlin would seek some classification. You must have good contacts, right?"

Perhaps I've done nothing wrong now. Why do you delve into

174

things that you don't know anything about? He starts to look at me strangely, I know that.

"Herr Colonel, do you think you could leave this unsaid, please? It would bring trouble to officers of the Zentralamt in Prague. It's not a big deal: we are like one big family. We stick together, right?"

So that's what I didn't expect. Now just calm down and keep your composure. Think fast, how to take advantage of this. Just think!

"Burger, Burger. Of course, we are a big family, but listen to what I say to you. This town has a special status. It is to serve the objectives which, of course, you know, and it is absolutely unacceptable," my voice rises, "to organize any schweinerei – which I do not want to talk about here – because this conversation has just ended! Clear? Is that clear?"

"Of course, Herr Lieutenant Colonel! It is clear. Very clear," he adds and slowly he begins to smile again, and that's a good sign. We're all finishing the goulash and a few Jewish girls begin to serve beer. From the nextdoor dining hall there's now a noise heard, the noncommissioned SS officers dispersing to their rooms or to their positions. The goulash was exceptional; I am sure I've ever had better in my life.

"You are a competent man, Lieutenant. If the negotiation goes according to the plan, a promotion for all of you is certain."

I've let myself loose a bit. It seems that playing the high ranking role suits me. Maybe that's why I got here. Perhaps I can even change a few more things. Right away, a hiding place for small children, a place I know of, occurs to me. Could I arrange a better place and also clothing and food for them? Perhaps some paper ... perhaps through Burger, when we're such good friends now. What, are you going mad, man? Slowly and carefully, just no hasty moves. It's necessary to get to know this place better, to understand how the Terezín system works. How long do such inspections last? A week, or am I expected to stay here as long as the children from Bialystok are here? Now that's the next thing I have to find out.

"So that's what I call a family, gentlemen. Here's to Herr Lieutenant Colonel of the SS, who thinks about his subordinates. To our dear Herr Inspector! Cheers!" That's how Burger gets rolling after the second beer.

"All right, all right. Let's get back to work. When is the next transport to Birkenau?" I turn the subject of our conversation. "Ah, Herr Lieutenant Colonel will not catch me out again. They are directed by an announcement from Berlin. Numbers and specifications – we do not decide about them here. If it were up to me, the transports would be leaving every day. And when not one Jew would be left here then I'd start on the Bohemians, one right after another, bim, bam, bang – gone! You understand that we have successfully created and maintained the outward appearance of a new family camp. I will show you how we have managed this feat tomorrow morning when I take you to visit our propaganda bureau. From there, we send regular reports of our work to the Central Office for Reich Security. Despite some rumors that may have circulated, we are very successfully managing to maintain tranquility and obedience among more than forty thousand people through directed letters written by the prisoners themselves, Herr Lieutenant Colonel. Do you understand? I am very proud of what we have accom- plished!"

"Describe these 'controlled letters' to me, Herr Berger, I am quite interested in what you're doing. You are writing false letters saying that everything is wonderful here?" He's settling into his element, and seems eager to tell me everything.

"What's actually going on here in Terezín? Is this town just a prison where Jews work in the factories and shops while awaiting further placement?" Despite his disciplined dining, in his excitement Burger has spilled some soup on the table and now it's running down his chin as well.

I'm beginning to feel a bit sick from his presence, but I think now that his self-control is melting away I can find out why I'm actually here.

"Not at all, Herr Lieutenant Colonel: after the train arrives at night in Birkenau, everyone gets on the platform. Our medical staff takes the children away from their mothers – which is accompanied by certain noisy protests – but they are told that each mother will receive several post cards and when they write down what will be dictated to them, they will get their children back. Then they can all go together to the washrooms, where they get new, clean clothes."

"Continue, please," I try to smile and thus convey collegiality, understanding, and perhaps even admiration for what he is telling me. I'm doing poorly, because have I started to intuit where the story goes. But I push that aside and manage a greasy smile. After all, I'm a Lieutenant Colonel of the SS, an elite player in this hideous machine. I mustn't forget this, even for a moment.

"Well, naturally Herr Lieutenant Colonel suspects our next move. So we move mothers slowly to an elongated wooden house that is clean and sweet-smelling. They sit around a round table and write everything that is dictated to them: that they arrived at a beautiful family camp, where they met with friends who left Terezín some months ago, that they have plenty of food and the children have toys, they have light work in the gardens and the workshops for a few hours a day..."

"And then?" I jump in on his speech.

"Within half an hour they are with the children in the showers. And then the gates just close after them. You have not been there yet, have you? What a wonderful place!"

"Close the gates and ...?" Burger starts to laugh loudly and after him his subordinates join in. I start laughing too. Then we form one long merry table in the lounge for officers, which other lower ranks don't have access to. Burger starts choking with laughter and it becomes difficult to understand him. He says something to the effect of the soot coming out of a steamboat's smokestack or something. Then I come to realize what he'd really said: they fly out the chimney. That's what made all of them laugh! They shut the door after them and instead of water from showers a gas will spread over them. A few days later beautiful postcards from the East with the positive reports of family camps are handed out here in Terezín, saying that they all manage to colonize the new eastern territories. So, after all, it is true. How else? For a while you believed those propaganda talks at the Neo-Nazi gatherings: that it's all a fiction made up by the Jews. They said that the numbers are fictitious and women and children were never hurt.

I have to figure out a way to help those little ones who are hiding in the underground cellars. Tomorrow I have to find that guy, what was his name, Jakob. I've got to help him with those kids as soon as possible.

"Heil Hitler, Herr Sturmbannführer!" All suddenly jump up and everyone gives the Nazi salute, while Burger rises noticeably slower. An SS Major unknown to me enters the room along with his assistants. Slowly, I also stand up. From the army I know that he's got to greet me first. I'm the senior officer, aren't I?

"Heil Hitler, Herr Obersturmbannführer!" The major

greets me and continues, "Welcome to Terezín, how do you like it here? Excuse me. Allow me to introduce myself, Major Heinrich Jöckel, the Chief Commander of the Small Fortress, prison Geheime Staatspolizei. I have heard you were here, so I said to myself I could come greet you and have a chat about what's new in Berlin."

That's not good at all. He acts too confidently, as if he had a higher rank, and has no respect. His prison is clearly not under my authority. But I'm a Lieutenant Colonel, which is certainly a lot higher than his rank. He's bound to turn out to be some insolent sadist – I'm starting to recognize the type.

"Perhaps I disappoint you but I do not talk about Berlin with everyone and you, Herr Major, certainly do not talk about your fortress either, am I right? And now, if you will excuse me, I have work to do," quickly, with an arrogant look on my face, I stand up. Immediately, so does everyone else, including the two commandants, which is even better. Perhaps I salvaged the situation. As that nasty Nazi said at the beginning: I have a reputation as a loner and a weirdo. But now I'm making that work for me, I tell myself.

"You know, Herr Lieutenant Colonel, at some places even the highest inspection is not sent. In my fortress it is I who am the commander and the inspector. Heil Hitler, Herr Lieutenant Colonel!"

So that's how it really is. This is where the arrogance comes from. Prisons with no supervision? They can do absolutely anything there. That won't be a nice place. Greet and get out, the faster the better: "Heil Hitler!"

I'm coming out of the house in the square when Jöckel's assistant catches up with me: "Herr Lieutenant Colonel, Herr Major apologizes for his behavior and says that you can count on his people. They will be here one hour before the arrival of

179

the consignment. Heil Hitler!" he turns around and quickly leaves again. Who can I count on? I'm already beginning to lose my bearings among these ghouls. I could sure use some kind of break. Today, it was all too much for me, and yet there will surely be more. I've got about three hours. This concentration's exhausting me. I'd like a coffee or, instead of that maybe I'll go to bed in my room with a view. Perhaps when I wake up I won't be here anymore. Why am I so exhausted?

A roar of motorbikes and trucks and then a round of shooting tear me away from the comfort of a sound sleep in my room facing the square. For a while, I have trouble realizing where I am and what's happening. But it doesn't take long to once more realize that I'm in 1943. It's not a pleasant feeling at all. Anguish and uncertainty vex me; maybe I take this too seriously. Back in the time to which I truly belong, I coped with my selfrighteousness by taking deep puffs of marijuana, a fragrant flower whose scent I could never deny myself. A scent which eventually cost me my little Maru. And now I'm here and what I'd like best is to crawl back into bed. It's a little after seven in the evening. Do I have to go there at all? I'll just say I'm sick, so they give me space. Then simply take a driver with a Volkswagen and go to Prague. Change clothes and disappear somewhere. What am I babbling about now? This trip to the Jewish prison, which is the whole town, is more to me than just a mystical weekend trip. I met my grandmother and saved her life, probably thereby saving my father's and my own in the future. I realize that I belong to those who are imprisoned here. Perhaps it's time I finally did the right thing. Perhaps it's me who has the opportunity to change history. God, that's just a crazy idea! But, on the other hand, to find oneself inhabiting the past isn't crazy? "Herr Lieutenant Colonel? Can I come in?"

Here we are, here we go. Pull yourself together, man. Remember, who you are and why you're here. You're to supervise the arrival and, hopefully the residence here of Jewish children from a small town in Poland that was massacred. Children they want to exchange for German prisoners. It sounds a bit like the plot line from a horror movie, but that's what the local Nazis expect of you.

"I will be outside in a moment."

Burger's already waiting for me in front of his car with a retractable hardtop. Even though it's the end of August, it's cold outside and there's a chilly drizzle falling. Through the square there's one truck rushing by after another and the trucks are full of SS. I realize they're from the Small Fortress that Jöckel mentioned before.

"The train is set to arrive in ten minutes, Herr Lieutenant Colonel. Jöckel's people are a little delayed, but why complain about that, right?" Burger announces with a chuckle. My patience within this role is wearing thin and I'm beginning not to give a damn about what he thinks or whether my behavior is starting betray me:

"Tell me, Herr Burger, why is there not an inspector appointed for the Small Fortress? Can Herr Jöckel really do anything he wants in there?" "Oh no, the Small Fortress has an inspector and Herr Jöckel has a superior. But they are all good friends, you know? That's how it should be, Herr Lieutenant Colonel, one big family. Without the approval of Herr Günther from Prague, no visit by inspectors can take place. They have no chance, simply put, to surprise them: no one would let them inside."

We're on the spot. Jöckel's people run inside all the buildings standing along the track and then they appear in the

181

windows. They block intersections, forcing people outside to go inside. Nobody but the Nazis must remain on the street. They even send the Jewish and Czech police behind the fence. I stand next to Burger and quietly observe all the commotion.

Jöckel's got his adjutant here. He's screaming at everyone and sending groups to their posts. He's deploying a man every ten meters along the track. It starts really raining and it's getting dark. The daylight is superseded by street lamps. Finally, everything's fallen silent and the station area fills with tension. The driver brings me a black leather coat just as the rain intensifies. Everyone is waiting.

The rain picks up, then calms again. After a while, it swells, then calms once more. Over two hundred Nazis pace behind the windows of buildings on the street along the route of the tracks, in front of the train station, in front of the entrance to the barracks, at every intersection and at every doorway. All the residents of Terezín must be in their homes or their workplaces. The streets are deserted; only one special train is expected. Those who are brought in here are what they call a consignment. I turn toward Burger, who smokes one cigarette after another. I start wishing I had one too, but the train whistles interrupts that reverie. From around the corner, a steam locomotive emerges into view, slowly braking as it approaches the station. One of the Nazis runs into the entrance of the barracks and shortly afterward comes out leading a group of nurses and nannies. He commands them to deploy along the access platform. The civil train is moving at a walking pace and stops at a breakpoint at the end. The SS men from Poland who are escorting this consignment open the inside door wagons and jump to the ground. They give a sign to the Nazis on the platform to make more space. Next, young women come out and reach in to help children inside to climb down from the high wagon stairs. Those I was sent here for begin to come out.

"Give me a cigarette, Burger. And just this once, do you also have a match?" I ask him, overcome by nervousness.

Finally, they're descending the stairs. The nurses who have come with them help them out of the wagons and organize them into lines. My time decelerates. I can see it all so incredibly slowly, in grainy, rain-streaked detail. Five-year old children in tattered rags. Then eight-year olds, ten-year olds and four-year olds. Some are barefoot, some half-naked. I notice how some of the kids wear Nazi jackets. Under those jackets, they are naked.

Bach's sonata begins to resound in my head, the one which accompanies the slow passage of time. I'm trying to focus, and I rub my eyes. I'm so exhausted. As if I saw ...

It seems to me that the nurses arranging the children on the platform and those who help the children come out are bright white – no, I'm just overwrought – as if they were ... At this moment, squinting into the lights through the rain, I can't tell whether the straps on their backs holding up their skirts are wings. Or if they might be angels.

Nazis stand around in black coats, hats set down low on their foreheads to shield their eyes from the rain. It's as if the children felt themselves to be in the presence of dark forces. They're afraid of them. They stand obediently in lines as they've been commanded. They're looking around and whimpering, but quietly, so as not to vex the men in black. They're pressing against one another, holding hands. After a few minutes, they're soaked to the bone and begin to shiver. I can feel a dismay that the Czech-Jewish staff can hardly hide. Many nurses cover their mouths.

Apparently they'd like to reassure the children, but the

children are also afraid of them.

"It will be necessary to send the Polish staff back with the train, and tomorrow thoroughly count all of them," I hear Burger announce, and I finally manage to accelerate my perception. For a while I was completely out. What is it he's saying? To send them back with the train? These kids know them, they're used to them. Why does he want to send them away? "What are you saying, Burger, why do they have to leave with the train? Who ordered that? It makes no sense – just look at how these kids are afraid of the Czech nurses."

"I understand you, Herr Lieutenant Colonel, but the order just came from Berlin. I thought you knew. They have to leave immediately. In no way should they mix with the Czech personnel. They will travel on to Birkenau."

Can I cancel an order like that? I don't know, but I can try. Just maintain composure. He will ask for a confirmation, he'll go to phone somebody, they'll want to talk to me. This won't work. I mustn't do anything to reveal myself!

"Birkenau you say. Then it's a shame to lose them. They would help calm the children down. Without them, the locals will have more work on their hands."

A few Nazis give the signal that the train is cleared out. Half of the street is now filled with small wet children who are trembling with fear and cold. Soldiers order the Polish personnel to get back on the train. Kids start wailing and crying.

Mass hysteria infects each one of the thirteen hundred. They don't want to let go of their nurses for anything in the world. They're tugging them back, begging them, and praying. An officer instructs the Czech nurses to intervene. They're gently and slowly trying to pry the children's little fingers from the Polish nurses' dresses. Now the warrant officer gives orders

184

to the onlooking SS guards to intervene, which they do in a brutal and uncompromising manner.

"That's enough! Halt! Let them be. Hold it! Lieutenant, command our people to withdraw immediately behind the corner. Now!"

"What, Herr Lieutenant Colonel? I do not see why they should leave their posts. We're not going to handle those little Jewish bastards with velvet gloves!"

I lose my temper. I can't stand by and watch as the Nazi beasts beat these small innocents. I can't accept that their guardian angels have sent them on a journey into this heart of darkness. I scream at the commanding officer that I'll immediately send him to the Eastern front, a known vulnerability for everyone serving in the quiet Nazi rear. I remember that from war movies. "The Eastern front" is for them clearly something terrifying when the SS cling to such a panicky fear about it. Perhaps they're afraid of the Russians. The train will have a greater delay this time.

"Listen carefully: Do you know who I am? Do you know why I am here? Those children will be treated as if they were made of porcelain, Herr Untersturmführer! Do you understand? Reply at once that you understand!" "I understand, Herr Lieutenant Colonel!"

"Very well. And you will now let the nurses from Poland accompany the children to the showers and assist them until they are changed into dry clothes and taken to their protected area. Do you understand me?!" "But that is against our orders from Berlin. They may not speak to anyone; they must depart at once," Burger objects. All right ... what can I do now? I begin to explain:

"Listen to me well. I represent Berlin here. Clear? You will give orders to the Czech personnel that they cannot speak a word to anyone in Polish until they reach the isolation area. Polish nurses will accompany the children to the showers, then to the isolation area and they will remain there, along with the Czech personnel, all the time. I repeat that for the last time."

"But it's against the rules, Herr Obersturmbannführer,"

"Herr Lieutenant Colonel, are you all right? Herr Lieutenant Colonel?!?"

I wake from a half-sleep, standing up. What, was I sleeping? Was it just my imagination? The train pulls out and the Polish nurses wave to the children from the windows. They depart with the escort that brought them here. The children slowly set into motion. They're soaked to the bone and trembling. I'm a coward. I couldn't do anything at all. My feet are rooted to the ground. Burger looks at me and says nothing. What are they going to do when they find out that I'm not who they take me for?

"What? I have had a fever for a few days. Stop gaping at me like a fish, Burger. I am not well."

Jöckel is constantly eyeing me. I sense that he suspects something amiss. I simply don't behave like a typical SS man. I have to do something! I've got to pull myself together and concentrate. I'll go directly to him. That's the way it should be.

"Herr Jöckel, thank you for your cooperation, but we will no longer need you here. Withdraw with your men to the intersections and keep a lookout for another hour. No one can go to the Bahnhofstrasse. Otherwise I do not want to see your men on this street. Is it understood, Herr Sturmbannführer?"

"Understood, Herr Lieutenant Colonel!"

"Departure" and "Heil Hitler!" are heard. That's a load off my mind. It's necessary to be decisive and uncompromising. If I'd been focused all the time, I could have saved the Polish nurses. If! But it's too late for that. Now all that is important is to protect the children.

The Nazis return to their posts along the street. The Polish children stop crying and whining, and they begin to line up into a long, raggedy queue and walk toward the barracks across from the station where warm showers have already been prepared for them. All of them hold hands and anxiously peer around, then obediently follow their new guardians, for no alternative is left but trusting them. The Czech nurses try to be as kind and reassuring as possible. On their faces there is evident consternation, mixed with regret. They have no idea where the children arrived from and what happened to them, but it's evident that they perceive the horror the children must have experienced.

We reach the hall on the first floor in front of the washrooms. It's deserted; not a soul anywhere. The nurses start to separate the sixty children who will be the first to shower. They explain to them that they have to take off the wet clothes they're wearing. I stand in the middle of an endless crowd that fills the whole hallway of the first floor. None of the children, nor a single nurse glances at me. I take a long look at them all. I look at the unbelievable and moving patience of the fifty nurses who are tirelessly comforting the children and stroking their wet hair.

My heart clutches up as I see everything. I think and think, what can be done for them? I think of Jakob's children underground, and it occurs to me that they might be moved at night to join this new group of Polish children. If I can get them there, surely they'll be taken care of. There'll be an exchange, they need them.

Something happened, and the children start to wail loudly. They refuse to undress, and the chaos ripples across the floor. The boys are moving around, but wat are they doing? They're

187

creating something like formations: I start to get it now. They're creating formations, taking hold of one another's hands and keeping the rest inside. In confusion, the nurses force their way through the crowd. They try to find out what's happening, but the children rebuff them and won't answer their questions. The smallest ones are rolling around inside the formations and pushing against one another. All of them sit down on their heels, hugging each other and huddling together. The ten-year old boys are determined not to let anybody inside their circles. Some of the nurses start to cry with desperation. Now they look at me, anxious about what I'll do.

Worried, they anticipate that I'll call the SS to restore order. They attempt to persuade the boys not to make trouble; they try to untangle the lock of their hands. But none of the nurses manages to do this. Thirteen hundred children now shout:

"Gas, gas, gas!"

The nurses don't understand, but I get it. In Białystok, they discovered everything. That's why the uprising took place, that's why the massacre happened. They've heard about the showers and the gas that purls out of them instead of warm water. Even the children have heard it. The bravery of the boys is moving to me – their resolute faces. I have to leave immediately, they're afraid of me. The nurses can handle it, surely, when the children will be in the hallway alone. No Nazi, no worry. I avoid the nurses and head for the staircase. I pass by clusters of children encircled by boys, when all of a sudden sweat pours over me and a chill goes through my whole body. I have to stop to make sure that I'm not dreaming; that this is not a mere hallucination. On one of those kids surrounded in the huddle which I pass, I recognize the face of my little Maria, my little princess. She sits on her heels and embraces a trembling little girl. Puzzled, I look back at her. Her eyes are red from crying. I gaze at her and still can't believe it. Is it her or am I still having delusions? Is it possible that someone resembles her so much? Our eyes meet and the doubts are gone. The shock in a child's eyes proves everything. I need to disappear right away! What would happen, if? I start walking on again. I speed up, but it's too late. Despite all the shouting and wailing behind my back I can hear a despairing cry and the scream of one small, five-year old little girl, who's trying to make herself heard over the crowd.

"Daddy! My daddy! Dad, take me from here, please! DAD!"

I run down the empty staircase onto an ever emptier ground floor. I've run away from her, I've left her! Forgive me, please. Tears stream from my eyes and hysteria has mastered me. I don't know where to go. What am I supposed to do? That was Maru, my child.

That's enough! This is not even possible. I want to get away! I want to wake up, this can't be a reality. Where am I? She was my dear Maru! I sit on the stairs of the empty ground floor. My head's in my hands and I'm desperate. It was her. Her voice, I'd recognize it anywhere. And she recognized me. How could she have suffered the same fate as me? How did she get here?

You've got to buck up, bud! Stop sniveling and get your bearings in this situation. They taught me how to survive in extreme conditions, how to adapt to the unpredictable. To spend a day and night in the water, to accept fate with no regrets. How to make yourself invisible; defeat an army of enemies – sure, but this? Is it possible to prepare yourself for a journey into the past and into this situation?

There's nothing left but to finally concentrate. First, I've got to feel my breath. I get it. I'm in a hostile environment, but I don't need to step out of the camouflage. I need not show any weakness to the enemy. I will not regret my own fate, but simply accept what it is. I get it. All right. Enough sobbing. I could use a cigarette. Now Jakob – I've got to find him! He'll help me figure out how to get out of here, along with my Maru too.

"I am looking for a Jew named Jakob, from the technical department. He should be an artist, and he is 19 years old. Get him now!"

After my order, the temperature in the workshop drops to the freezing point. Everyone looks at the ground. I guess they're Jakob's friends. They're worried about him. I look at everyone one by one, to see if I recognize anyone from the tunnel. I'm not sure. I sit at a table and wait. I'm beginning to get used to this role, dangerously well. Where did he say we were? What was the name of the barracks with the cellar full of children? After all, I've got an idea how to help them. So where is he stuck? Hopefully, they won't come back to tell me that they can't find him. There's not much time left!

"Herr Lieutenant Colonel, I have brought Jakob. Is he the one you are looking for?"

"Yes, and now get out and go about your business," I take Jakob aside to the passage where the entrance to the workshops leads. Thankfully, not a soul is anywhere.

"Herr Lieutenant Colonel, or Paul, what do you need? I thought they had come for me to tell me I should go immediately to the workshops. You have no idea how relieved I was when I saw you."

"Listen to me, Jakob. I'm sure you know that thirteen hundred children came here from Poland. Right now they're all, one by one, having showers and receiving clean clothes. Berlin's negotiating a ransom with the world. Eventually, they'll be sent on to Switzerland or Palestine, somewhere safe. I'm sorry that

190

I'm talking so fast, but it upsets me. Well, you must understand, one of the children is my little Maria."

"What? Do you think one of them is your child? This can't be possible; how did she get among them?"

"Slowly, Jakob. I don't get it either. Trust me, there's no point in trying to figure out what's going on. What I need is for you to help me get her out of here. And myself as well. I'll have a car; I need to go to Prague. I need contacts for the Czech resistance. Somewhere to hide, and survive for less than two years."

"Two years?"

"Yes, Jakob. In May 1945 the war will end. Jakob, listen to me carefully. There'll be six million of you dead in the end."

"What six million, Paul?"

"Six million dead Jews, Jakob. Six million dead Jews. Nearly the whole Jewish population of Europe is going to disappear. They've been killing you for years in the forests of the East. There are entire factories of murder. Do you understand this? It's not just one place, as you think. There are hundreds of them. The only ones who survived are those who fled, those who were hidden. Don't hesitate if at all possible – there will be large killing sprees at the end, too. Prepare the tools you'll need for a wagon, then open it from the inside and jump out somewhere. In Poland there are a lot of partisans in the forests."

"What are you saying, six million? How is this possible? It can't be!"

"Will you help me with the little ones? Jakob, are you listening to me?" "Six million? So they want to kill us all! I thought the majority were in labor camps."

"I'm sorry, Jakob, it's hard to hear this but now I need you to tell me if you can help me. Will you work with me?"

191

"Yes, I will. Our network has contacts with the Czech resistance. Paul, swear to me that I can trust you, that you are who you say you are and it's not just a trap. I'm sorry, but it just doesn't make any sense at all. The guys from the leadership were saying that you just want us to trust you and then you'll round us all up. But I want to trust you."

"Tell me, does the underground passage lead to the barracks opposite the train station?"

"Why do you want to know? Why are you asking me this?"

"Wait, it's not like that. I know that sounds wrong, just calm down and listen. Thirteen hundred children, one by one, are showering. It's assumed that it'll take at least another two hours. If a corridor was leading to the cellars of the barracks ... the time has come to save those children you're hiding in the cellar. Tell me, do the corridors lead to the basement of the barracks across from the train station?"

"Yes, of course. They run through all the buildings, or almost all of them." "Excellent. I want you to trust me, Jakob. I sent all the SS men to the junctions. In front of the building and inside it's deserted now. The children were terrified of the officers. Inside, you'll find nobody apart from the thirteen hundred children and the nurses. People are waiting until they are all washed and changed and then they'll pass them along to the isolation area in the corner of the city. From the cellar you'll get to the first floor and order the children into a line. Their counting will take place no sooner than tomorrow. I don't believe that the nurses will report anything. Can they be trusted? What do you think?"

"I know who they selected for the children. A lot of them volunteered for the job: they would never say anything. It's an excellent plan, Paul. Only we will have to break through the walled entrance. I'll take care of that; I'll get the others to help with some tools. This has got to work out. Thank you for what you are doing for us. I trust you. If this works, I will do anything to help you get out of here. Maybe even with your little girl, anything."

We shake hands and look one another in the eye as an affirmation of our mutual trust. Quickly, he then disappears into the darkness of the hallway leading to the workshops. It will be midnight in one hour. I have to get back to the station. I'll check if the SS are guarding the intersection vigilantly. This is going to work out – it simply has to.

I was concerned that the Nazis would be irritated by having to keep watch outside for so long but, surprisingly, they don't seem to be. Jöckel apparently went back to the Small Fortress and Burger slipped away to his office. Only adjutants have remained, and they wouldn't dare object to the SS Lieutenant Colonel's orders. I start to feel calmer. Not a soul is anywhere in the barracks. All who live at this address remain throughout the night huddled in the corridors of the other barracks. This night's gonna be a damned long one.

Jacob and his crew manage to break through the walled entrance to the underground. It's impressive how quickly they manage to organize everything. Not even twenty minutes has passed since our conversation in a hallway at the workshop, and now a group of grubby children, accompanied by Jacob and his friend, is running up from the basement towards the first floor. Success. After another five minutes these two young warriors gallop back to the basement. We pass each other on the ground floor. I stand at the half-closed front door and through a crack I watch to see if one of the Nazis hasn't taken the notion to approach. Jakob comes running up to me, shakes my hand, and tells me what's going to happen next. "A plan for hiding you in Prague is being prepared, don't worry. Every night one of us is on duty in the workshops. For the men of the resistance you're a hero, they won't ever forget this. When you arrive there, they'll send for me. At the top I spoke with a nurse about your daughter. Don't worry, I revealed nothing about you. Apparently, there's one tearful five-year old girl who speaks Czech and says that she saw her dad in the corridor. I told her to take very good care of herself and told that nurse not to let her out of her sight. Everything will turn out all right. You should go to sleep, at least for a few hours. You're looking haggard. Early in the morning, pick your daughter up and bring her to the workshops. Have the car ready; you'll get the address where you'll be safe and the two names of those who will arrange documents for you within one week."

I can't believe it. How could they do that? They're locked up in prison and yet I feel that whenever they wanted, they could disappear with me. Yet for others' sake they'll stay. They're capable and so much needed here – true heroes. I'll remember them.

"Great, Jakob, great. I just wish Maru and I could be out of here already. You're right; I'm so exhausted that my eyes are closing standing up. I'll go to bed. At four in the morning, the whole city will be fast asleep. I'll pick her up from the isolation area and come out in front of the workshops. Wait, did you hear that?"

Burger's taking someone with an escort. Some group of men in white coats. "Quickly, Jakob, get out of here. Run!"
"Well, Herr Obersturmbannführer, here you are. So what about our little Jewish mice? Are they quiet? We need to take a proper look at those vermin before moving them on."

"Not now, Herr Burger! The children should not be scared away now. You will wait until they are settled in. Leave it for tomorrow."

"But, Herr Lieutenant Colonel, after all..."

"Depart, Herr Burger, at once!

Burger takes me aside to the stairs, away from the door, and quietly says, "Terezín's nice doctors can easily wait until they are all settled in. How long can it take, till two in the morning? We just need to ensure that no local white coats talk to anyone, you know. Our four people will be sufficient to check that they have no infections. You know that we need them to be in top condition. Come on, Herr Lieutenant Colonel, it's no big deal. No one will stand over them with a machine gun."

I don't have the strength to resist; I've run out of arguments. I can't think clearly. I don't know what's an acceptable compromise to the plan and what's not. I need to close my eyes, at least for a while.

"Very well, Burger, your four men will guard your doctors, but without weapons. They may go through the quarters, but they may not order them to make lines again. Clear? I am going to bed now. Aren't you?" "I'm as fresh as a German goldfish, Herr Lieutenant Colonel. I'd better keep an eye on everything personally to ensure they are securely locked up."

Yet a scenario floats through my head, "Doctors and their examinations". We've all seen such things in movies, and they haunt our nightmares. I imagine these four guards who accompany them. I don't envisage anything that might risk my morning getaway with my daughter: getting out of here and never coming back! We'll begin a new life in Prague. All we have to do is somehow survive until the end of the war, then we'll emigrate to England.

Where am I? It's half past three, I slept like a log, maybe three hours. That will have to be enough for now. Just get yourself together and put your clothes on: the uniform. My head is feeling a little dizzy, but let's recap. Step 1: pick up the car. Here we go. The guard is sleeping in the hall, his head resting on the table. For a moment, it occurs to me not to wake him up, but what if he was to wake up and find that the keys from the Volkswagen are missing? He'd get frightened and start to panic. When he reports that I've taken it, it will look odd, but ... I've got it!

"Guard, on your feet!"

"Herr Lieutenant Colonel, I ... I'm sorry. I fell asleep just now, but only for a moment. I changed with the first guard at 3 o'clock. Accompanying the doctors among the children was exhausting! I apologize."

"All right, Corporal, I will not report this to anyone. I need to go to Litoměřice town to see a certain lady."

"I understand: you want me to wake up the driver. Wait a moment, I will find out which one is on duty."

"No need, I will drive there myself. I will be back around noon. Just give me the keys."

"You do not want the driver, Herr Lieutenant Colonel?"

"Come on, Corporal. Certain discreet visits do not require witnesses, man."

"I understand: I'm sorry. Of course, it's all right, take these," the corporal hands me the keys.

"And the examination of the children, how did it go? I hope everything went smoothly?" I ask.

"Essentially, yes. Only about thirty of them failed. You know, defective pieces. They just took them away," the Corporal tells me.

"Wait, what do you mean that thirty pieces 'failed'? Who and where did they take them?"

"Well, those doctors, they labeled about thirty children as substandard. They had infections, tuberculosis, or high fevers. If they left them there, they would infect others, so they took them away. Herr Lieutenant Burger ordered it, he was there too."

"As if he would miss it. In which part of the hospital, which floor?" I ask. The corporal begins to smile, his face distorts to an aberrant expression. I still don't get it for a few seconds, "Where ... did ... they take them?

"To the Small Fortress, Herr Lieutenant Colonel. Where they will be beaten to death like the rats they are. In fact, perhaps it is already over." God, these vile animals! How could they? Get Maru out as quickly as possible! Keep a calm expression on your face.

"I do not recall granting permission for that. Tell Herr Lieutenant that when I come back at noon, I want a report about it."

"He did not want to wake you, Herr Lieutenant Colonel. He said that nothing else could be done for them, and they would all bite the dust soon in any case. Because of them we would have had to guard another room in the hospital, perhaps an entire floor, and also be susceptible to infection. It was the best solution, don't you think?"

It makes me want to shoot him on the spot. Or maybe break his neck, since a shot would wake everybody up. But the corpse with a broken neck would be found at six in the morning. The best thing, then, would be to calm down, pick up the little one and try to forget these atrocities.

Everything goes smoothly, not a soul anywhere. The smell in the air foretells that we'll encounter more rain on our journey. I guess that when we get to Prague, it'll be 6:30 in the morning. We can easily melt into the city's early morning rush. I try to recall illustrations from history books, but I just can't imagine the living reality of Prague in 1943.

I arrive at the entrance to the area surrounded by barbed

wire. Oh! I was expecting Czech officers, but the SS are standing in front of the wicket. I totally forgot that he told me the elite SS reinforcements had arrived. Should I just take her and hide her in a blanket and bring her to the car? No, no, not like that. I'll tell a nurse to hand her over the fence from the other side. Is there any road nearby? I don't know. Damn. I should have asked Jakob to help me with this. I'll go for him. He's waiting for me in the workshops. But no, that's madness! I turn now when they see me? Tell me what to do, for crying out loud. But, no to that too: here I'm the one who gives the commands. I've got the power to do anything I want – so I play it pretty tough.

"Heil Hitler, Herr Lieutenant Colonel," "Inspection. You, come with me and take me to the nurse on duty. Two of you remain here. Now show me the way!"

I pass some oblong wooden houses and head up to a small lighted cabin at the very end. I try to obtain a look at the landscape behind the wire fence. In the morning twilight, I make out the silhouette of the walls. In front and at the back there's a deep ditch. Going this way, I wouldn't get anywhere. It'll be necessary to go through the guards.

What am I going to tell them when I take her to the car? I just won't tell them anything. Wait, I thought of a little scenario. I'll put her in the back seat, then approach them and promise them a promotion or reassignment to Berlin. I'll take their names, so it looks legit. This might do. I should have worked out more details with Jakob. There was no time to create a better plan.

"Good morning! Do you know who I am?" In the cottage, two nurses are asleep at the table. As soon as they hear me they jump from their chairs to stand upright. They're scared to death. One of them wants to say something to me, but she's not able to utter a coherent sentence through her quivering chin.

"Calm down, please. Everything is in order. I just want to take a five-year old Czech-speaking girl who was looking for her father yesterday evening, before the showers. Do you know which one I'm talking about? Did Jakob tell you that I'd come for her? Come on, so speak! Jakob, did he talk with you?"

"Is that you? You are her father? Jakob said you were with us, for heaven's sake..."

"Don't worry, nothing will happen to you. If Nazis come in during the day, simply say that you had to give her to the SS Lieutenant Colonel, you know? Nothing can happen to you. Moreover, the real counting will be done today."

"But she is not here anymore. They took her to the hospital along with the other twenty-six sick children; she had a very high fever. She kept saying that we should let her dad know she was here, that he would come for her. We thought she was delirious. With the others, there was a suspicion of tuberculosis. They were taken away about half an hour ago. You'd need to go to the hospital if you want to get her. But she's really in bad shape, so they'll want to put her to bed."

"What are you saying? They took her to ... ? God, no!"

"Jakob, you've got to help me. You said that the Small and the Large Fortresses are connected by underground tunnels. I need to get there. Right now, Jakob. You know these corridors well, take me there, will you?!"

"I will, of course, I know the corridors, but why don't you have your daughter with you? What happened?"

"Jakob, my little Maru's there, along with twenty-six other children. There's not much time left for them, those brutes want to beat them to death like rats, do you understand me? God, maybe they've already murdered them, but I mustn't think about it. Maybe they're just locked up somewhere but still alive. They must be! Just take me there."

"Paul, think for a minute. How do you want to help them? Even if I lead you there, you'll still be there all alone. This is suicide."

"Stop doubting, Jakob, and take me to the damned tunnel, you understand!?"

"Whatever you say. Come with me, we have to go through the tunnels to the South Wall. We'll go around the two police patrols. The first one will go fine, he's a decent man. He helps us. Before the second one we have to do a little play acting. You'll be scolding me or something. Let's go: if we run through the tunnel we'll be there in ten minutes."

It goes exactly as Jakob said: he knows it here very well, every corner, every patrol and tunnel. With a quick step we approach the southern rampart, he unlocks the painters' workshop, and we go through it and go down the stairs to the basement.

"Wait a minute, there'll still be lamps somewhere. Give me some light, please." He rummages through a cabinet full of paint cans; he's nervous and things fall from his hands. I'm a lot more nervous. Adrenaline is flowing through my whole body. I start to get cramps in my face, and my hands are sweaty. I have no idea where I can find the children; I only know that I've got to get there. She'll be scared to death, hoping and praying that her dad will appear at the last minute. I can't disappoint her again. The idea that I'll arrive late makes me shudder. I try to push it from my head as much as possible, to suffocate it; this option is out. Today, I'll kill for the first time. I'll take as many as necessary. It can't be that hard.

"Here it is. I was afraid that I wouldn't find it, and that would severely delay us. In the tunnel, there's complete darkness. Take it, so we can both run fast in the tunnel."

"Where's the damn tunnel, Jakob?" I'm losing my mind.

"We need to push aside this big wardrobe."

At the other end of the room there's an old cupboard. We lean on it – and a barred entrance appears, similar to those used in old cities as the entrance to a sewer. He unlocks it with a lock pick. From the darkness, more steps emerge leading deeper underground. We turn on our flashlights and set out running. Everywhere there's a damp musty smell. After about five minutes, we run up to a crossroad of two tunnels.

"We now continue straight. The second tunnel would bring you to the forest, more like a small grove. Behind that, there's a dirt road," Jakob pants, "up to now I was wondering how to help you. I admit, I think that we won't see each other again. That mission of yours is impossible, they will kill you there. But, still, I wonder: if you manage to get the children back here through the underground to this second tunnel, about a half mile from here there's a passage through the old cellar of a small waterworks. It's all overgrown with bushes and hasn't been used for many years. I'll be waiting for you there. After I lead you into the fortress, I will run back. It'll take about ten minutes before I reach my party, then another ten minutes. A man who has an acquaintance in Bohušovice will arrange for a truck to be loitering on a dirt road behind the woods. We've got good contacts with some of the locals. They'll help us, you'll see. I believe that in an hour everything may be ready."

Jakob is kind. Half of what he said I didn't understand as we were running, I only know that if I manage to get to the crossroads of the corridors, we won't run straight, but we'll head right and follow it up to the end. There, he'll be waiting for us with a ride. I don't need to know more. I'm not thinking about anything other than killing the first Nazi. Some, maybe, would say, "a man," but for me they're no longer people, just as they don't consider the Jews to be people. If I am going to kill them it's better not to consider them as human beings. It seems that we're here.

We crawl over a fence, and the tunnel behind it expands to a larger room, perhaps a dungeon. Jakob quickly unlocks it with his lock pick. A candle placed in a small hole in the wall illuminates only a small part of the space, and I don't see the body which in no time I trip over.

"What's in here?"

"Careful, we're not in the place yet. That's a room where Germans live. But you don't need to be afraid; they're already half dead. They won't give us away."

I don't understand what I'm seeing, but it doesn't matter right now. They're sprawled everywhere. With the flashlight, I shine light in all corners of this hole. Some of the old ones are awake. They sit huddled together, and in terror squint in the sharp light of our torches. Slowly, we step over the sleeping bodies and we slowly get closer to the dark tunnel to reach another barred entrance. Jakob locks it behind us and I once again run the light over the whole dungeon. I just want to make sure that apart from the old and dying German Jews, no one else has seen us.

"So, how much farther, Jakob? How many more rooms like this?" "No more. If we hurry up, we'll be there in five minutes."

He's right, after a brisk trot, bars appear before us, through which we can't see further.

"We're here, Paul. Now, we just push aside this huge wardrobe and we're in the basement of the garage and technical rooms in the first courtyard. The second courtyard was recently finished; it's full of military prisoners. They'd hardly take them there. I'll pray for you. I still don't know who you are, but I feel privileged to have met you. You're a good man, coming in here out of nowhere to help us. If you manage to free them, you know where I'll be waiting. You have incredible courage."

"Thanks for everything. Please take care of the details as quickly as you can. With luck, everything will go smoothly and I'll have them out soon." Jakob fixes me with a disbelieving look one last time, then turns around and starts running back into the darkness of the tunnel. I crawl through the gap between the wardrobe and the wall to another cellar – the last one. My flashlight illuminates the space and I search for something, anything, that might come in handy. The light seems to be fading: but if the batteries run out I'm going to be leading twenty-seven children through pitch darkness, so I'd better do what I have to quickly and make it back before that happens.

At the top of the stairs I find a door, which, unsurprisingly, is locked. Jakob's pick doesn't work for me, but it's no wonder, given the way my hands are shaking. Instead, I pick up the bayonet, a solid piece of iron, and smash it against the lock, which now gives way easily. Quietly, I enter a small room with windows, dimly lit by the lanterns in the prison yard. As I sneak towards one of the windows I notice a little table with a lamp, next to a narrow couch. Is this a guardroom? It reminds me of military school, except that we lounged on a ripped-out bathroom door instead of a proper divan. The doors leading out to the yard are open. A guard might come in at any moment, or, he might not, but I'm not going to wait and find out. Taking a deep breath, I head out into the courtyard.

Everywhere it's dead quiet, I can't see any guards. It's time to pull myself together. Stop being nervous, I tell myself. If I can maintain a professional icy calm, this will just be an event like any other. Here I've just got to add the ending – to kill. They've got my little girl and I've come for her. So here I am. I have no idea where they've taken the kids. I don't know where to go. A clap of thunder bursts into the dead silence. That's good. The roar of the storm will drown out whatever noise the killing makes. There's no more time for hesitation: it's time to act quickly if this mission will succeed. Along the walls inside the block I quicken my stride; as much as possible, I have to move within the shadow of the ground floor fortification buildings. This is one of the ways of making myself invisible. There are no guards anywhere, only a few of the illuminating lamps. Where's everybody gone, somebody's got to be on duty?

There he is! I finally reach the first one. Picking up my pace, I career straight into his back. Another lightning flash, and another rumble of thunder come just in time. As I begin to sprint, the echo of thunder disappears and my footsteps can be heard. But I've got good speed. He frantically turns around and my wide-eyed expression meets with his. He's in shock and has to breathe before he can scream. But it doesn't come to that.

My knife slits his throat in half as I sprint past him. I have trouble stopping and then I throw myself to the ground like a soccer player when he misses the ball. His body slumps lifelessly to the ground ... another flash of lightning followed by powerful and loud thunder reverberates. I hurry, but I don't know exactly where.

I run along next to a wall, and now, again, I go back to the Nazi ... he's got a dagger ... I take it ... the rifle's useless, it would make too much of a racket, but there's also a bayonet, so I take it.

Where to go now? What to do with his body? I don't know, I

don't have time to drag him somewhere, I don't know which doors are unlocked, I don't know the path of the patrol, I don't know anything at all that I need to know now. What the hell should I do? The nervous panic has come over me again. I've just killed the first man ever in my life. No, he cannot be considered a man, he was a helper of Satan ... excrement; no, something worse. A powerful man prepared to beat small defenseless children to death. I pray with all my might that it's not too late.

I've beaten up a lot of people in the past, broken their arms, dislocated shoulders, shattered knees in a couple of fights, pressed Adam's apples down throats ... once, I messed up a couple of punks real bad. But they were always trying to hit me or someone I cared about.

It's different here. My hands shake, I don't know where they've taken the children. My Maru's with them. Perhaps it's not too late yet: just think a little. Where would they take them? Constantly, the same thoughts plague me.

I overhear voices coming from around the corner: another patrol. They walk along the wall and get closer to me. I cling to the wall. I've got to time things right; watch and wait. Breathe calmly. A moment later, a leg appears, then a hand, and then his head. Then a second passes and he turns to my side. I take a second dagger. The sound of the gravel my boots crush on the ground is getting louder. So come on. Just carry on. I press my hands around the knives so hard ... it must pass through on the first attempt, as when breaking a brick using hands... simply pass through on the first attempt ... as quick as possible ... and here he is! ... Leg ... hand ... head ....now! Fast forward lunge! I slice right through him like butter. A huge hole is opened up in his neck, from which blood sprays in all directions. The moment I pull out the knife the blood spurts out to cover half of my face. His nearly lifeless body still manages to take a lunge back and push the second SS man to the ground. He glares with a crazed look in his eyes, and clumsily tries to catch the falling body. Before he can summon a whimper, I'm at him... I throw knives over in my hands and without self-control I furiously start stabbing, in a choppy way, at the SS man's head, into his chest ... and again at his head. I stab the already dead body with a hole in his neck. I don't know why, I find it hard to control this ... and then start again driving the dagger into the body of the first one. Blood sprays on the walls, on the ground, and in a few moments, there's a giant sticky red pool.

My uniform is now sticky with a red liquid smelling of Nazi bodies; it has to come off. Quickly, I undo all belts and buckles. I hurl the jacket into a red puddle, I'm lighter this way ... and I'll definitely be faster. I don't consider the advantages of wearing a SS uniform. There's no time to think through anything. When I go with the children on the truck, the uniform of a high-ranking officer could come in handy. What an idiot I am! I can not stab any more, but then I catch a new wave of energy and continue the mindless slashing and cutting. I'll need a jacket, maybe a coat of some sort ...

Two bodies lie before me, which through my frenzied stabbing, I've separated their heads from their bodies and drastically opened their chests ... Perhaps I was afraid they'd pick themselves up again, I don't know. I kneel down and watch, still out of breath. Slowly, it begins to rain. I knew it. Thunder and lightning come at ever shorter intervals. This is going to turn into a blessedly deafening storm. Suddenly, I remember that these children are seriously ill. They have high fevers, pneumonia or tuberculosis. How are we going to get them to run two kilometers through the dark tunnel? I begin thinking of everything that I could have done differently with the advantages of my position. I could have run to Burger and given him an order for the children to be drowned in the river like unwanted kittens rather than beaten like rats. I'd start laughing in front of him and he'd be sure to join me, he'd buy it. Once we were together in the truck, I'd quickly and quietly slit his throat. It wouldn't be a problem then to also get rid of the other four Nazi ghouls who would probably be accompanying us. Anything could serve as a weapon; I'd improvise with whatever was on hand.

If only I'd managed to stay calm ... the God of "ifs" floats before me sticking His tongue out in mockery. Who would do be able to do that? Knowing that a child you love will be beaten to death along with other little ones like her ... come on, calm down, I've got to go on. I'll keep on going in the shadows along the walls. I can't kill the next one; he has to tell me where they've taken them. The patrols, of course, would have to know that. A small truck drove them here; the patrol will know where. I can't kill him, I can't kill him. Calm down. Breathe slowly.

A somewhat heavy rain turns into a downpour. I'm soaked to the bone. All of a sudden, a siren starts to blare piercingly across the Little Fortress. Is it over? Someone probably ran away. Soon, I realize that it's because of me. Probably other patrols came upon the mangled bodies of their colleagues. I'm like a stone, frozen to the spot. I can't decide where to run. Back? There'll be loads of them now; but what if not? Go further forward? One by one, all the lights are lit. They can be heard. From the direction of where I came, a lot of voices are coming. Black jackets emerge from the heavy rain. I don't see many of them, but I hear the barking of dogs, many dogs. And they already see me.

207

From all sides I hear: "Don't move. Raise your hands!"
I get away from the wall and little by little I head to the middle of the yard. I'm not going to raise my hands for you. Twenty, maybe even thirty SS in black coats are screaming at me. But there is something wrong: I can no longer understand German. My head starts to feel dizzy and everything seems to slow down. Through the thick piercing rain, a pack of enraged German Shepherds are lunging toward me, barking ferociously. The first canine warrior leaps for my face. I manage to dodge it, and it flies to the side. While it regains its balance and turns back around one of its packmates hurls itself upon my legs, I kick with all my strength into its open muzzle, which was ready to rip into me. The bloodthirsty beast whimpers, but looks around to the others for reassurance.
I want to draw my handgun, but it's slippery. Never mind, screw it: I still have two SS daggers. Considering what they did to those three watchmen, they'll help me take care of these four-legged assassins. The beasts spring on me from all sides. From the slow-motion perception, everything speeds up. As each one lunges, I stab it with a dagger and then quickly withdraw it to get ready for the next. I turn to face the direction of one of my attackers. It's one of the dogs that already once succeeded in biting me. I yell out in pain and in three seconds I cut off its head, but its teeth are still buried in my calf.

I glance up and take notice of the black coats laughing, they're enjoying this. They surround me in a semi-circle, sticking to a distance of about ten meters. Another cur leaps onto my back and tumbles me down. One of the daggers slips out of my hand and there's no time to pick it up again. I strive to stab with the other one with all my strength. Yet another dog bites me in my high boot and furiously wrestles his teeth into it. I can't stand up. The beast that missed me the first time throws himself on me again. I manage to hit him in the neck. I can feel the wretched animal taking my boot off. As they gain confidence, they use their teeth more efficiently, biting deeper and holding on tighter. I keep using the dagger, but it's too late: the pack is getting bolder and the number of bites is increasing. Adrenaline fails, and a wave of exhaustion washes through my body, leaving the pain in stark relief.

The slaughter seems to last for ages, and I notice a puddle of blood pooling up behind me. Still, I stab and cut at them as best I can. Eventually, those beasts that survived surround me, but only growl ferociously and do not press a further attack. They've got stab wounds, some quite deep. Weighing their injuries along with the agony and death of their pack mates has changed their minds about continuing. Around me are lying about seven German Shepherds, some missing legs, two without heads and the rest with bleeding stab wounds. I barely manage to get up from the ground, when a burst from a submachine gun shatters my thighs and knees.

For a few seconds I'm not even able to shout out, the pain I experience is so intense. My legs buckle down and I fall back into puddles. Finally, I succeed in breathing and let out a fierce hysterical scream which drowns out even the heavy downpour. I writhe in pain and spasms and slip into a strange trance. I completely cease to feel my legs, as if they never existed. I watch the lights slowly go out; the rain hasn't stopped, it only eases.

They pull me across the whole yard, through puddles and mud, and up to one of the ground level buildings that has a huge wooden gate on its side. Most of the black coats leading dogs keep their distance from those who are dragging me, but they also head to the opposite side of the yard, somewhere around the corner.

They come to a halt in front of the gate and one of them starts opening it. "Gibt es hier, was hat Herr Obersturmbannführer gesucht?"

I manage to translate a few of his words in my head. He's asking whether I was looking for this place. Suddenly I black out when the SS man abruptly treads his heavy muddy boot on my face.

The strange thing is how, just before I pass out, a scene flashes in my mind when, at one event with the neo-Nazis, I knocked out a Jewish bodyguard, who was trying to protect his group as best he could. I had stepped on his face in just the same way.

As the gate creeps open little by little, creaking, the moan of weeping children can be heard. I was so damn close. In the middle of a smaller yard, lit by a single lamp, a cluster of drenched small children is clutching each other, singing a Jewish song with tearful voices:

"Un der rebe lernt kleyne kinderlekh Dem alef-beyz..."

Around them, a circle of black-clad servants of Satan reel about. They laugh and bloodthirstily gaze upon the little bodies. The children, once they notice the bloodstained man being dragged, fall silent. They all gape, looking at me. I writhe in a pain I hadn't even felt until now. One of the SS men kneels down to the children and smiles at them pleasantly.

"Well, come on, you stopped singing, that's not the way. This way you won't get to your little beds. So continue: one, two, three!"

A song is not what he gets, but the opposite: the children start crying – loudly and desperately. They hug each other and bury their heads in one other's shoulders.

"Sing! I told you to sing, you filthy rat spawn!"

He stands up and looks at me: so it was you who cut up my men! How would you like if we cut off your bullet-riddled limbs, hmm? Drag him over to the children!"

Well, man up, I tell myself: stop feeling the pain. I wish ... so many things I'd wish for. For example, to turn back the hands of time and be a better man. Where are you, Maru? I don't see her anywhere. The children turn away from me. Maybe she's somewhere in the crowd. Your daddy's come to save you! Look, your dad's a hero – who messed up absolutely everything.

"Maru! My Maru! Daddy's here! Hello! Where are you?"

"Daddy!"

God, she really is here! She wants to pull through the crowd of children, but she can't. They're grasping each other too tightly. I can see her. She's a little way away from me. Confusingly and desperately she cries: "Daddy!"

I try to move, but I can't. To move a little bit closer to her, to have a chance to hug her for one last time. To protect her with my own body. To do "something"!

"Get to work!" sounds from the shadow in the corner of the yard. Jöckel, that sadistic beast. I know what he means when he says that to his men. So this is how it ends. Not able to do anything, inches from my little princess. Forgive me, girl. Your dad was a preposterous, conceited fool. He thought he'd be strong enough to beat the whole world.

The black coats step closer and it all starts slowing down. This time, and for the last time, I look at her and she's crying. Crying and shaking, and I cry too. I try to shout; I still resist. I try to draw myself up with my hands to the crowd of frightened, soaked and weeping children from Białystok. Desperately, and in vain, I swing my hands, when the servants of Satan himself are using rifle butts to crush the little bodies

211

of the future angels. I no longer hear their appalling shrieks, because I've just become mad. I yell, roar, screech – but not a sound comes out of me. With my mouth stuck open in a frozen roar, I stare at the murderers.

They point at me and I can hear their laughter as if coming from a far distance. Eventually, everything goes black, as a rifle butt cleaves my skull. I can see the white light that all of us have heard so much about. It's pouring through me, and I begin to feel lighter.

Take me with you, Bubu. Don't leave me here. Please! Please!

Beep ... beep ... beep. Slowly, I open my eyes, everything's blurred. I hear a regular sound being emitted from an electronic device of some kind: beep ... beep ... beep! Something white appears in front of me and then next to me. I become aware of the modern institutional fluorescent light on the ceiling; then make out a picture of a snowy landscape on the wall. Is this a tube in my nose? Everything hurts. Slowly, I move my left hand. I move my right hand, but I can't make a fist. Where am I? White coats, it's...

I'm in the hospital. A modern hospital. What am I doing here? Where's my Maru? I'm ... "Lie still, Mr. Batel," a nurse soothes me, "Doctor, he's waking up."

"So I see. Great, Nurse, give him a high-dose B12 injection. We've got him back."

"Where is my daughter? Maru. I didn't manage to save her. Maru was ... what year is it?"

"Excuse me?"

"What year is it? Tell me, what year is it?"

"Don't get up, stay lying down, sir. It is 2005. You've been in a coma for several weeks," the surprised nurse informs me. "Doctor, he's looking for his daughter."

212

"Well, that's strange, there's nothing in his papers indicating that he has a child."

"My Maria. My little Maru."

The nurse gives me another shot and pulls out the tube from my nose. Then she turns over my pillow. I can smell her perfume as she leans over me and I feel weakness, fatigue, an overwhelming exhaustion. It was just a dream, it was all just a dream. My eyelids are falling, it was just a dream. Thank you, God, thank you so much. It was just...

"So, we have you back," the doctor welcomes me, "At least, I hope so. The last time you came to we lost you again! You slept for two days after you woke up from the coma and after that we administered a replenishing infusion. Now it will be all right. How do you feel?"

"Everything hurts, especially my legs, doctor. I don't understand – it was just a dream."

"What dream? Did you have a bad dream? I'm sorry to hear that that. People do not usually experience dreams in a coma. Do you even know what happened to you? Do you remember anything?"

"The professor wanted to show me ... wanted to show me something. I can't remember."

"You were climbing into a hallway in Terezín and you fell into a deep pit. An old wooden floor broke under your weight, and it took hours before they pulled you out. You were unconscious, completely battered. Your body had bruises and lacerations, broken legs, broken ribs, and you lost a lot of blood. It's actually a miracle that you survived all that. What were you thinking, climbing into a place like that? Were it not for the old gentleman who noticed you going there, you would not be here anymore. It was he who summoned help: you owe him your life. Nurse, pull out his artificial feeding tube. Thank you. Well, now, just relax and eat. The fractures healed well; after rehabilitation you will be up and about again just like new. You'll be a strong man again. In fact, all that muscle mass helped you by cushioning the fall onto a hard surface. I'll come tonight to check you again. For now, just rest."

So I had fallen down a shaft, and the rest was just a dream. But the pro- fessor did have a key, it was him ...

"During the last few weeks, you've had several visits. They seemed very interested in you."

"Nurse, please, tell me, wasn't there a five-year old girl who came to see me?"

"Certainly not, I would have remembered that. But different guys were coming in to see you, and some of them were kind of scary. One time, six or seven of them came together. The whole department was talking about it, about who you might be. Also, that older gentleman came every other day. He was last here yesterday, but you were still asleep."

"The old man?"

"Yes, the one who helped you out of the tunnel."

"Nurse, tell me, please, what's the date today? What day is it?"

"It's Wednesday, October 5th."

Wednesday. That means I missed my day with Maru. I have a whole month to wait before I'll be able to pick her up again. Damn tunnel! What might they have said about me when I didn't show up on Monday?

"Why do you keep asking about the date?"

"The date means everything to me, nurse. If you only knew what I was dreaming about and how real it all felt. So very much alive ... "

That night, I didn't sleep well in the hospital; I had nightmares. I was dreaming about killing someone somewhere in the Bavarian hills. I did it quickly and quietly, just as I was taught

214

back at military school with the boys.

"Good morning, Mr. Batel, may I come in?"

"Professor?"

He sits down quietly and slowly on the bed and is silent. Did he bring me there on purpose? After all, he had the key. What did he want to show me in that tunnel?

"How are you doing? Are you feeling better?"

"I was in a coma for several weeks." It's hard for me to talk, I'm still battered. He's come to see me, the professor. I wonder whether or not he has any idea what I was dreaming about.

"You got lost on purpose, professor, didn't you? You recognized who I was."

"Yes, Paul, I did."

"You were also in that procession, is that right?"

"In what procession?"

"In the Old Town, when the neo-Nazis attacked the Jewish parade. You just said that you recognized me, so you had to be there too. I had a scarf over my face, but you recognized me all the same."

"You mean the attack by the neo-Nazis? It was all over the news. Lots of injuries, terrible. I was not there. You were with the neo-Nazis? Were you also beating innocent people?"

"I'm a security guard; actually I was a guard for their leaders."

"Very interesting. And do you no longer do this work?"

"I quit, I'm not gonna do it anymore."

"Why? Don't they pay you well?"

"What kind of questions are these, professor? Why are you here? You led me into the tunnel on purpose, and then you vanished. The doctor says that I lay unconscious and injured for several hours before help came Did you want to scare me or kill me? Just where in the hell do you know me from, anyway?" I go on, irritated, "And why did you want to get rid of me? Have you come here today to see if you can finish me off?"

I want to get up, but I immediately get a prick in the side. My head falls back onto the pillow. I've never been so badly battered.

"Now I'm slowly starting to understand, but nothing is dawning on you yet, Herr Obersturm... It's all right."

"Obersturm? Did you want to say Obersturmbannführer? What is all right? What is not dawning on me?"

"Why have you quit working for the neo-Nazis?"

"I still haven't, but I will. They just don't know it yet. What should I tell you ... that I was angry at Jews? That if a bloody Jewish immigration officer hadn't taken offense, if he weren't so sensitive about his Jewishness, I could have, when I now leave the hospital, gone for a walk with my father and with Maru? If that corrupt judge, the Jewess, hadn't taken her away from me? Huh? Jesus, what am I babbling on about? ... I'm sorry." Suddenly, tears flood my face. I'm oversensitive, probably from those pills they're giving me here. Memories of my father touch me every time. No matter how much time has gone by since then ... and this forms a heady combination with my thoughts of Maru. I can't keep it up. The professor looks at me, and says nothing. Why has he come anyway?

"You have a daughter, Maru? How old might she be?"

"Five and a half. I'll see her again next month. I missed the date this month because of my fall into the tunnel, professor. Why did I climb in there with you?!"

"I'm sorry for that. Does it mean you are now going to hate the Jews even more?"

"What are you talking about? Go away, professor, go away! Now I have to figure out what's going to happen next. My head is full of questions. Leave, please."

"Just tell me, why are you quitting? You know, it's very important for me to know this."

"I don't want to work to protect evil anymore, I won't serve it. And now, please, just go already."

"They have not agreed with anybody."

"Sorry? Who hasn't agreed?"

"We believed that they would survive; that they would send them to Switzerland and then to Palestine. We believed that they would get their captives and they would agree."

"Who ... what are you?"

"If only you saw them, they were so cheerful. They were playing for whole days on end and they had so much food that they couldn't even eat it all."

"I don't understand you. What are you talking about, Professor?"

"You really don't know? Truly? One morning, about a month and a half later, they were all gone. I remember how we, on Yom Kippur, uttered a prayer for their safe journey. But precisely on our holiest holiday, they murdered them in Birkenau."

"Wait, you're talking about..."

"You know, Paul, I have never forgotten you. For all the men in the resistance movement you were a hero. We believed so much that you would succeed. If only we'd had guns and a little more time to prepare we would have attacked all together.

I was waiting for you at the water tower and when I heard the siren and the gun shots, I knew it was over."

"What are you saying? For goodness' sake, that's just not possible."

A chill crawls all over my back. I'm shaking like a leaf and tears flood my eyes again. The professor takes my hand and presses it gently. In this unbelievable moment, not a single word escapes me. The moment, which changes forever my up-to-now-confused and empty life:

"Jakob!"

It's a touching moment. After more than sixty years, we meet again. He's telling me about the shock when he recognized me in the uniform of a private bodyguard. He's telling me about the secret in the tunnel which he understood only after the war when he found out about the things he couldn't have seen in '43. All those long years, he held onto the key that opens the way to the tunnel I had come through back then. He took me there and waited for what would happen. Only now, I've confirmed that the tunnel's real. He's saying goodbye to me. He's saying he's a tired old man.

He leaves an old tin box next to the table by my bed, saying I'll know what to do. He's leaving. For the last time, he stands in the doorway:

"Don't let them forget their story, Paul!"

I gaze out the window and all the thoughts have disappeared from my head. I'm not thinking about anything, just staring into empty space; just like when I was a little boy waiting for my papa. I was trying not to think about anything, about the time I figured out that too many thoughts make me sad. He wanted people not to forget. Don't be afraid, Jakob, I won't let them forget – I won't.

Days roll by. I eat hospital granola and corn flakes and slowly gain strength. Lying down, every day I try to lift each leg up and down a few centimeters, at least a hundred times. Then, a few minutes after my strenuous exercise, I fall asleep. I think about my little one, looking forward to our next meeting. What might she be doing now?

"Well, well, can this even be possible? Who do we have here? Well hiya, you sick little puppydog. We lose him in one of those damned Jewish tunnels and he falls into a hole. When we heard the news you should've seen what it did to us."

The wind's playing with the leaves on a tree. The sparrows hop from branch to branch. In the park, there are children playing with a ball and moms sitting around on benches, rocking strollers and chatting. The peace and quiet of this place fled, and a cold feeling of nihilistic evil was seeping throughout the room. If only I wasn't in such a battered condition.

"Go away."

"What? Look, Herr Heinz has stopped by to look in on you personally. Do you know what an honor that is?"

"I said, go away!"

"What's wrong with you, Paul? Don't you want to see Herr Heinz? What's gotten into you, man?"

"I don't wanna talk to you. I'm not working for you anymore. Leave me alone."

There are three of them, and in the doorway there's a bald one watching, someone that I don't know. I think he's my new substitute. Herr Heinz, whom they call their leader, is there too, and Heinrich. I know they've got weapons and that they'd also easily be capable of chucking me out the window. I know that here and now is not my time. If only I had my gun. How can I get rid of them?

"You're saying you don't work for us anymore? But don't you know that no one just walks away from us?" Herr Heinz reminds me.

"Herr Heinz is right, Paul."

"Be quiet, Heinrich, and wait for me in the hall; give me a minute alone with Paul."

Heinz sits down on a chair and wipes his little scarred and sweaty face with his hands: "And now, tell me, why do you want to leave? We don't pay you too little, so it isn't an issue of money, is it? It probably has a ... deeper subtext: is that so, Paul?"

"Yes, it has a deeper subtext, Heinz."
"Have you forgotten what the Jews did to your father? Just why you have a right to hate them so much? It's your duty to take revenge on them." "My father died because of me; no Jew has anything to do with it. I just blamed it on somebody else so I could look at myself in the mirror. Jews aren't really at fault for my father's death; I am."

Yes, this is how it is. I couldn't imagine living without the benefits that my life in America offered. I could have gone at any time to help my father: I knew how dire his situation was. Instead, I kept sending him messages to hold on. It was unthinkable for me to leave the consumerist, materialist country where I had everything. And what was it all for? I'm not going tell him this, but perhaps he'll understand when I tell him:

"I actually have Jewish blood. My grandmother was Jewish, so, in fact, my father was also a Jew. Now I know I was working for the wrong side and I have nothing in common with you! So just go your way and let me be."

"Wow. Yes, a betrayal in the true Jewish style. Look, look. Do you understand what you're doing? This means that from now on, you're our enemy, Paul. Tell me ... do you really think that you'll walk out of this hospital alive?"

I'm ready. It would be enough for him to lean over me and then I'll break his neck. If he just moves a little more towards me it will be close enough to grab hold of him. I'll use the pen that's tucked in the pocket of his jacket against the two bald gorillas. I know they don't have any knives on them, or silencers for their weapons. They'll want to suffocate me with a pillow, or throw me out the window. Just come at me, Heinz!

"What are you looking at me like that for? You're not gonna say nothing? After all I've done for you? Hmm, a broken, abandoned little Jew has crawled out of your skin and shown us his true colors. You were once one of our own, a proud warrior, but from now on you have no family, no one's gonna give a damn about you. I'll see you in hell, Jew!"

I don't utter a sound. Silently, I watch him go to the door of the room where, unfortunately, I am lying alone. He's going to be after me from now on, though it seems there is a shadow of regret: he'd actually rather not have to. In a moment they'll be back, it's just a pity I didn't grab that pen. I quickly scan the room for anything else that might serve as a weapon. How much can I actually move? At the door he turns around; he looks like he wants to say something, but instead, he just shakes his head.

The door closes behind him. Now is the time. In a flash I'm up on my feet. Come on – you're not crippled, and the bones in your legs are no longer broken. What's a little pain now compared to what they're going to do you if you don't get out of here? You've got to set yourself in motion, so get off the bed!

I notice a few hangers in the slightly opened closet. I'm interested in the wooden pole the hangers are on – that might be useful. I heave upwards and take my first steps after having spent several weeks in bed, and immediately fall on the floor. I grab at the desk, but it topples down with me. An almighty crash accompanies my cry. My legs are simply too weak to carry me. Quickly, I sit up on the floor so at least I can face the enemy.

"Hey, what's going on in here? Christ, who told you that you can get out of bed?" the nurse swears, rushing into the room with the doctor. God, what a relief. Both try to lift me off the ground, but I'm just too heavy. "Hana, go for the others so we can lift this heavyweight back into his bed."

"Doctor, the people who are loitering in the hallway are very dangerous. Are you carrying a cell phone with you? Call the police! There's a suspect wanted by Interpol among them; I recognize him!"

"What are you saying? There's no one in the corridor."

"There isn't?"

There really isn't. You made a mistake, Herr Heinz, and when your gorillas come around next time, I'll no longer be here. And when you'll seek me, I'll be the one who finds you instead. The doctor kneels at my side and doesn't know what to say. I notice his name badge: it says David Stern, MD.

"Tell me, doctor, is Stern a Jewish name?"

"Yes, Stern is a Jewish name. Why might you be asking?"

"And tell me, Dr. Stern, will one Jew help out another Jew who's in trouble, even in these times?"

"What do you... you bet they will!"

Before the ambulance drops me off in the city center with a wheelchair, it stops by my home in the building behind the station. For five hundred crowns, the driver goes to pick up a few things for me. One of these is my unregistered, illegal gun. Another is the old sweater with pockets that my grandmother made. I told him how important it is for me to have it, and he didn't forget.

Another five hundred crowns, and the ambulance driver learns to recite a meaningless address at the end of town (in case, by some chance, anyone asks); and the ambulance quickly moves away from the pedestrian zone. Not being able to walk, even if only temporarily, is a terrible feeling. People usually look elsewhere as soon as they glimpse someone in a wheelchair; it's an interesting experience. I roll through the whole pedestrian zone, cross the square and several other blocks in my old sweater from Grandma. I stop in a narrow street behind the church, through which only a few cars go during the day.

I don't wait for long, and a taxi driver who passes by is even so helpful that he helps me climb inside, and despite our language barrier, drives me where I direct him – two kilometers from my well-thought-of hideout. With my fluent English I pretend to be a foreigner. He guesses I'm a Dutchman, and I flatter him by letting him think he was right, so as not to leave anything to chance so close to the end game. I like autumn evenings, and I really cherish the freshness of the breeze as I make my way toward my new shelter in the wheelchair.

Finally, I'm safe. I know very well that no one is going to come looking for me here, because nobody knows about this place. Miky passes me a lighter, smiling, and I light a cigarette. The one right before a meal has a really good taste. In a while, we'll have dinner together.

"It's goulash tonight, bro. You'll really dig this."
Miky's happy, tomorrow he'll show me the local gym, and, after so many years, we'll be working out together again. Here, I'll find true peace. Here is where I'll prepare myself for my new mission.
I fall asleep in a room at Miky's, but before saying good night, I tell him one incredible story. He smiles in the dark room. Miky has always liked my stories. In my hand, I'm clutching the tin box from Jakob and I've got my grandmother's old sweater pulled over a pillow. An inside pocket full of cash wrapped up in a rubber band presses against my chest. And I have a little metal friend, one without a number. But that missing detail doesn't bother me one bit. This secret friend now keeps me

company as I drift into sleep. Peace and quiet ... peace and quiet ... peace ... and peace.

"So you see, Mom let us have the whole weekend. Isn't that nice? We're going to take a trip, sound tempting?"

"Ohhh, a trip – where are we going, Dad?"

"We're going to Slovakia, where we'll sleep in a mountain cabin. They rent out bikes there and they've got a swimming pool too. Edible mushrooms grow in the forests, and we'll also fly in a balloon – do you want to try that?"

"Oh, a balloon, I've never flown in a balloon! That will be amazing!"

"I have a friend there from the army; he's looking forward to meeting you. On the way, we'll stop in the town where my Dad grew up, before he came to Prague."

"To Bratislava?"

"You remember that? Aren't you something! You made my day, Bubu; I'm so happy."

"Dad? And what job are you doing now?"

"Now I tell stories."

"And what are those stories about, Dad?"

"About what can happen when people stop being nice to each other." "And what can happen then?"

"Evil can start to take over. And people gradually start to serve it, and then they start doing nasty things."

"And you, like, tell those people not to be mean to each other?"

"Well, I rather tell them what happened long ago, when evil started to rule over people, and what happened when they stopped being nice to each other."

"Dad why don't you tell me everything that happened? Because I would be scared?"

"Exactly, Maru, 'cause then you would be scared. They were

very nasty things."

"All right then, and when will we be there?"

"We're here, Bubu. We're here."

"It's so nice here! And it smells lovely."

"That's the scent of the trees. Pine, you know? For miles around, there's nothing but pines. Come, first let's buy some flowers in that shop over there, some special ones. We'll choose them together, OK?"

"OK."

It always takes me a while before I find the place where the tombstone lies. The cemetery stretches up into the hills of the pine forest. The Little Carpathian Mountains begin here. I can't get here as often as I'd like, it's over three hundred kilometers from Prague to Bratislava. A few years have passed since my last visit, and today's one is exceptional because I've brought my little princess with me. Papa would have loved her. And Grandma and Grandpa? I'm sorry that I didn't spend more time with them. Fate planned things a little differently.

"Well, put down the flowers one by one. That one'll be for your grandfather, this one is for your great-grandfather, and this one – this one'll be for your great-grandmother, dear, kind Zdeňka Raabová."

Without you, Grandma, I'd be completely lost. That day in that living room you were right: not all of them were bad. And maybe it's only thanks to you that I wasn't.

"Now help me find some little stones." "Okay. Large or small ones?"

"Just right, Bubu."

"How many?"

"Three. Find three of them. Do you see any?"

"I've got them. And why do you need three stones, Dad?"

"We'll put them next to the flowers. This one is for my dad, this one for Grandma and this one for Grandpa."

"Dad, but why are we putting down the stones? We have given them the flowers already."

"So they'll have it nice here. We put down the stones to honor their memory. Grandma and Dad were Jews, Maru. A long time ago, when the Jews were wandering through the desert and someone died, they couldn't put flowers on his grave because there weren't any growing in the desert, so they started using stones."

We have a great time in the mountains. Petr Novak, my old friend from academy, is excited to meet me again. True friendship isn't affected by the passing of time, and we pick up exactly where we left off fifteen years ago. The weekend passes by quickly; madly, as madly as it can when you're having so much fun. How little is necessary for happiness. A cottage and a camp fire. When Bubu sleeps, me and Peter have a serious talk and prepare a serious plan.

A trip in a balloon over the forested mountains is prepared for the other day. How lively and thrilled a little girl can look when she's experiencing these things for the first time.

The whole journey back she sleeps in the car. I wake her up when we get closer. Her mother is waiting for us on the street in front of her house. I carry her into the house. Lucia speaks to me, though I admit, I'm not listening much: I look at my little Bubu.

"We're going to see each other soon, Maru. All right?"

She starts to cry, silently. I hug her and whisper:

"Just don't forget, I'm with you all the time. I have you here inside all the time." She lays her small palm on my chest and hugs me again.

"You are with me all the time, too, Dad."

I leave and feel fine. A month will pass by like nothing. What is a month? Time means nothing at all. I'm looking forward to that wonderful weekend, and then, it'll only be like this for another year. When that passes, we'll be together again. I can't even describe everything that'll happen then.

"So, we are here."

"Siegfried, goddamn it, listen to what I'm saying. Nobody must recognize who we are and why we are here. It's an exceptional excursion. Our brother's ancestors operated here and fulfilled the tasks the Führer ordered. Now we're about to follow in their footsteps and taste the past. Look around you and imagine them as they were – standing proud all around here and doing their jobs like honest men. This trip for the new-bies was planned by Herr Heinz and poor Heinrich. If some Jewish beast hadn't taken them down in Bavaria, they'd be here with us now. This trip's in their honor! Clear?"

"Commander, let me speak."

"Cadet Helmut, bloody hell, we won't address each other here in our normal way. We're an English-speaking tour group from Berlin who are interested in history. Talk like that, and you'll give us away!"

"I'm sorry, teacher."

"Well, that's it, as we agreed. You're from the institute for troubled youth, the English class, and you're on an educational trip. That way they'll tolerate some greetings, or behavior that wouldn't seem appropriate for Czechs. But, you mustn't overdo it!"

"Teacher, I would like to say that it is an honor for me to be selected for this trip. I'll write a paper about it and present it at the next convention." "Well done, Thomas. I knew that you are one of us, even if your physical condition doesn't comply with the standards for admission. We need a good speaker and promoter really badly. Listen for every detail, because we're coming back. The NSDAP, our party, is growing, and you're our future elite. You understand that?"

"Good morning. I am your guide and you must be the group from Berlin, is that right?"

"Sir, you came in as quietly as a ghost. I must admit you made me jump! Of course, we're that group. But excuse me, could we speak privately a moment?"

"Yes, of course. What's going on?"

"You know, these are troubled youths; they have experienced various kinds of trauma in their childhoods and as a result, some have behavioral issues. If you could be tolerant of their sudden strange outbursts, I'd be very grateful."

"This is due to their upbringing, you're saying? Um, of course I understand that."

"Well, I admit that I was expecting a different ... a more intellectual- looking tour guide – but, man, you are pretty athletic! Do you go to a gym somewhere?"

"I once trained a lot, but don't judge a book by its cover; this bulk is mostly just my jacket – I wear it because it gets cold in the underground areas. Once in a while, I overhear a group a comment from a student about "the spectacled fat man" and so on. I'm used to everything, so no worries. Let's get started: please follow me."

"Of course. Students! We are getting started, follow our guide. And behave yourselves!"

"Let me welcome you to Terezín. We are standing in the town square. It did not always look like is does today; it used to be surrounded by a high wooden fence, like most of the long streets.

Like this, the space in the city was even more cramped. During this period approximately 40,000 Jews on average were staying in the city. Whole families lived here, but also elderly Jews from

Germany and Austria, who didn't have anybody here. Therefore, they suffered in this Czech Jewish town, surrounded by walls. Men were separated from women. Children older than 8 years were separated from their mothers.

But before I even begin to tell the story of the Second World War, we must first carry on to the end of the 18th century. There, the story of this city, misused by the Nazis and soiled by their deeds 150 years later, begins. Long ago, in 1780, the Habsburg Emperor Joseph II....

"He's good, the fat Czech dude, right?"

"Whisper more quietly, so he doesn't hear you. He's a thick, spectacled sissy."

"He thinks he's so damn important. Hey, how about we take him down somewhere?"

"Jesus, Helmut, you asshole. We're here to educate five of our future elite SS men, not on a training raid. That, of course, is being planned again, but not today and not here."

"Hey, why are we whispering, you said that he didn't speak German," Heinz replies.

"...cause you never know. Got it?"

"Three SS commanders operated in Terezín – Siegfried Seidl, ..."

"Here!"

"Siegfried, behave yourself! Please excuse him,"(the "teacher" grumbles). "... Anton Burger and Karl Ram. Burger, a former professor from Vienna, despite spending only half a year here, belonged to one of the worst groups of Nazis. He was a sadist and a psychopath. When he was drunk, he and some of the other SS men used to invent sick ways to have 'fun'. Sometimes they sat down in a truck and drove through the streets of Terezín until they encountered a group of Jews that was moving in an organized manner across the streets between the wooden walls. They sped up the truck as much as possible and drove into the group at full speed. Their victims, primarily elderly people, or small children accompanied by a teacher, would panic and often didn't manage to jump away. Then there might be six or seven massacred bodies lying there in the street. From the truck, which kept going, a loud laugh was always heard."

"Free reflex training."

"Excuse me, do you want to ask a question? You must do so in English. I do not mind if you jump into the story and have questions, I'm used to it. So, what was the question?"

"No, that's all right, sir. He was just quite shocked. These things you're talking about are horrible, especially that Herr SS Lieutenant Burger." "Good. I see that you have previously studied some things about Terezín: that's excellent. So whenever something is unclear to you, just ask. What, for example, most piqued your interest when you were reading about this city?"

"I haven't read anything. Just go on talking. Why did you think I read something?"

"...cause our teacher's also a pervert. Ha, ha, ha."

"And also well-read."

"Siegfried, Dietrich. Enough! Where's your discipline, cadets?" (The "teacher" admonishes them in German)

(in German language) : "Excuse us, Commander. Sorry, it's not going to happen again. But don't worry, this chump doesn't understand a word. From now on, we'll be model students."

"Life was stabilized in time. Everyone knew where the rest of their family lived and after returning from factories, or after the end of working hours, they visited each other. It was not easy, however, since there was no privacy here. Jews here had no place to be alone. At eight o'clock in the evening in winter and at nine o'clock in summer they all had to be in their places of residence. Some lived in large rooms in the barracks, some in the corridors, while others dwelled in local family houses. Surprisingly, life in those houses was even worse than in the former military buildings, which at least had an extensive drainage system and large shower rooms built in."

"Yeah, showers! They expected nice warm water, ha ha ha!"

"Wonder if they still have a supply of cans of Cyclone B, huh?"

"Excuse me for jumping into your conversation, but I understood from your German: Cyclone B. Yes. The Nazis really had a small warehouse with Cyclone B here. They also had a gas chamber built. The local Jewish resistance, however, was ready to blow it up in a moment if and when the Nazis had decided to use it. The Jewish resistance was made up of brave young men, on average 17 to 25 years old, like you are now.

A separate story could be written about them. When they found out what was happening in the East in the so-called "family camps", they smuggled guns and grenades into Terezín. They were ready to fight and they had worked out a plan."

"How could they find out? Someone probably gave it away."

"Could you speak English, Mr. Dietrich?"

"Here!"

"You remind me of someone, Mr. Dietrich. Let's go to into the museum for a moment."

"Well you know, guide, sir, it's not that we aren't interested in museums, but could we see something real instead?"

"I didn't mean the ghetto museum; we will move to the Small Fortress, the Gestapo prison. The local museum has an exhibition on the local Nazis. Everyone who was of any importance in Terezín. I think you will like this."

"Hear that, boys? An exhibition dedicated to our own. So we'll like that, what do you say?"

"Commander, he's looking at you so strangely, as if he understood. You'd better be careful."

"Thomas, you won't cry here, will you? Keep your comments for the chat room and shut up."

"Pardon, Commander, it's just that you yourself said it. I'll be quiet."

"Judging by how closely you're examining the photos of the SS officers, I get the strong impression that you are really deeply interested in World War II. I am also very interested in that period, but I have admit that telling the story of this city is sometimes tiring for me. There is much more to show and to tell; for example, the whole ingenious system of fortifications."

"Wow, I knew he'd be a whizz. Boys, now listen carefully. The guide is going to change the subject for us."

"Sorry, what?"

"I just told them that you are going to pick up another page of history. They'll like that. You know, they are all a bit upset from the whole story." "Yes, it is a depressing story. I myself am interested in the weapons that were used in wars."

"I knew you would have to be a militarist."

"So will you show us the fortifications?"

"Of course he'll show them, Dietrich. He's cut from the same cloth, our guide. I was saying to myself that his short-cropped hair had to mean something."

"You know what? Let me show you something real, places where soldiers were waiting for the enemy. Where they served their shifts, where they slept within the walls when there was the threat of an attack. I will show you the underground world of halls and tunnels inside the fortifications."

"This guide's really different, Commander."

"I'm quite impressed, Kurt. It almost seems like he was – or could be – one of us. Excuse me, I'm telling them how lucky we are to have encountered you. You've been a wonderful guide."

"Yes, I'm also glad that I have, after some time, an ... atypical group. We are approaching the ramparts – see? People easily overlook it. Or maybe they ignore it because of they are so preoccupied with the whole story of Terezín – and yet these walls hold so many of their own secrets and mysteries."

"And here we are."

"Oh, that looks like a scary entrance. It's too bad we can't go in; but still, thank you for showing us something others do not have a chance to see." "This is only the beginning. Come on."

"What do you mean, guide, sir? You mean to say you can get us through those bars."

"Precisely. I have a key in this box that an old man once gave me. It is very valuable, and it's a secret that belongs to me alone."

"Commander, that's just amazing – let's go explore!"

"Not so fast, guys. Wait, there's no light here!"

"Don't worry about them; they'll definitely stop and wait for you just around the first corner."

He looks at me and finally becomes serious. Something's becoming clear to him:

"You are not an ordinary guide, are you?"

"I'm not, and what's more: Ich verstand alles, was Sie gesagt haben."(I did understand everything you were saying)

"What, you understood us the whole time. So you know..."

"I would have known even if I didn't understand German. I never said that Burger was a Lieutenant of the SS,

233

'Commander'."

"What are you doing? You've lost your mind! What are you going to do with that gun?"

"Your cadets are already on the other side. You shouldn't leave them alone there for too long – they might get into trouble. Go!"

"You're a psycho, man! What's in that tunnel?"

"As Jakob said, 'The day will come when you will be held responsible for your actions, sir! Then see if you find courage around you. If you proudly bear the consequences of your hatred.'"

"Jakob who? I don't know any Jakob. Isn't that a Jewish ..."

"I'm telling you for the last time, GO!"

"Don't kill me, please. I'm going – you see that I am. You won't shoot me, will you? How far should I go? I can't see a thing. Hello? Hello! Hell..."

Farewell, future Nazi elite. Now you'll see clearly what you are so blindly praying to. You exercised your free will to serve this evil; so be it! Just go back in time and look at your heroes.

I sit on a bench near the abandoned, rack-and-ruined Hanoverian barracks. I take one cigarette, of course. How strange it tastes, having only one each day. This is, I think, the right time for it. A moment for a personal sin. There are so many: like sending those young men to the other side. Playing Mr. Righteous; the one who has the right to mete out punishments for others. Look at you, man! You sit in this godforsaken park all alone. You'll go home, to your bunker in the attic, and you'll sit there alone. A few weeks more to go before the weekend of weekends comes and you'll pick up your daughter. Maybe they'll call you from the travel agent's office to do another tour of Terezín. Perhaps not even that. Perhaps nothing at all.

I'll go home and I'll stare at the wall. I'll sit in the armchair and, after a while, turn on my favorite show with Larry David, the one I've seen a thousand times already. I'll try to laugh at least a bit.

Perhaps I'll write to some female: send her a message that I'm alone and hoping for some company. And maybe I'll get a response after three hours or so, because they seem to feel that this guy is weird in some way. True loves are long gone. I'm tired of getting to know new faces in bars and clubs. I'm tired of training people who have no talent. Every once in a while I let them hit me in the face so they can feel that they're doing a good job. Perhaps I'll go have a walk somewhere, but what for? All those places, I've visited a hundred times. Meanwhile, women that I'm genuinely interested in avoid me, because I'm a not a suitable catch – just an oddball who likes to talk about his daughter, and who is bitter when he realizes that it bothers them.

What'll happen next? I don't feel like sitting in a chair and listening to the radio. I don't feel like hammering away at a punching bag or a wooden dummy only so I can endure matches with my trainees. I don't feel like teaching people who are without passion for the cutting-edge fighting styles I've picked up, piece by piece, all over the world. I don't feel like running up into the woods and kicking a tree. Or jogging up the hill, at the top of which I'll light a cigarette anyway.

Loneliness is killing me. Waiting for the beginning of the month is an endless torment. This life, in brief, just doesn't make any sense to me. Who are those lost evil souls going to recognize on their journey into the past? What loved one are they going to see die? What will the tunnel prepare for them to pass through? Something that will change them forever I believe.

You were also like that, alone and lost in the void. You hated the whole world. You blamed everyone and everything, but just not you yourself. It took you so long to find out ... that you didn't understand anything. What have you just done, man? Who are you that you can send them to hell? Was this the professor's order? To take revenge? Nope, not bloody likely, buddy. And they haven't gone to their deaths, but to a new awakening. You've just come to understand and it's gonna take a few more puffs of the cigarette before you admit it to yourself. You already know what your mission is: yes, I know.

My boot stamps out the cigarette butt. Rising up from the bench, I head to the bars. I don't feel like it, I admit. It's not easy to go back, if you know what you have to go through, but I just can't leave them there alone!

We each have our own little missions, our role in the history of mankind. A smaller one or a larger one. Mine's somewhat unconventional, I guess, but it's just as important as yours and everyone else's. What is essential is that we understand the roles we are to play, and whom and what we are going to serve.

I can see the little boy I used to be, and after all these years, at last, I'm ready not to balk and to pass through "the valley of the shadow". I lock the old rusty bars behind me and step off the ledge into the darkness of the even darker tunnel of the gate of time, because my name is Paul Batel and my true mission in life ... is to be a real guide.

Let this book be a memento to all young men who are lost wandering the streets and feel that life is not and has never been fair. Boys in adolescence, who have found the courage to run away from home or a detention facility, become an easy target for recruiters offering a new membership in neo-Nazi families that can never be left later.

Let this book be a memory of the story of the Białystok children that has been forgotten by the world and the city that once used to be called...

"Theresienstadt".

Pass this story on, and perhaps at least a few more will understand why telling it was so essential to me.

... dedicated to my "Papa"

ABOUT THE AUTHOR

Terezin guide, historian and writer Pavel Batel survived a violent childhood in communist Czechoslovakia. In the chaotic post-communist period he graduated from a military academy, and then entered the world of elite protection services, where he often had to save his clients from the kind of violence they were inflicting upon others. In surprising turns of events, Pavel discovered and identified with his Jewish roots during a visit to the Terezin concentration camp. This opened his eyes to the problems of ethnic bigotry, and he vowed to do his part in opposing the nationalist groups that were growing to prominence in the former eastern block countries in the 1990s. He truly makes the past come to life through his gift for storytelling. In the Tour Guide's Tale, Pavel tells the story of his past, and brings forth some of the most dramatic - and little known - historical events that played out in Terezin.

The Tour Guide story is told as a personal awakening, with the use of fictional bridges to past times and places, and elements of magical realism to heighten the drama. It is the author's hope that this work will not only entertain readers, but will bring greater awareness of the threat that hatred and intolerance still pose to our societies. It has been recognized by Philosophical faculty of Charles university as an exceptional and unique work of art.

Made in the USA
Middletown, DE
27 September 2023

39569152R00149